Editor
Sara Connolly

Editorial Project Manager
Elizabeth Morris, Ph.D.

Editor in Chief
Sharon Coan, M.S. Ed.

Illustrator
Howard Chaney

Cover Artist
Brenda DiAntonis

Art Coordinator
Kevin Barnes

Creative Director
Cjae Froshay

Imaging
James Edward Grace

Product Manager
Phil Garcia

Publishers
Rachelle Cracchiolo, M.S. Ed.
Mary Dupuy Smith, M.S. Ed.

For Kids

Primary

Author

Amy Gammill, M.Ed.

Teacher Created Materials, Inc.
6421 Industry Way
Westminster, CA 92683
www.teachercreated.com
ISBN-0-7439-3832-1
©2002 Teacher Created Materials, Inc.
Made in U.S.A.

The classroom teacher may reproduce copies of materials in this book for classroom use only. The reproduction of any part for an entire school or school system is strictly prohibited. No part of this publication may be transmitted, stored, or recorded in any form without written permission from the publisher.

Table of Contents

Table of Contents *(cont.)*

Student Activities Section

Table of Contents *(cont.)*

The Internet: A Classroom Resource

The Internet is a powerful resource that YOU can bring into your classroom. Bring e-mail pen pals and online dictionaries, math games and interactive maps, online picture books and online museums, as well as many other high-quality educational experiences to your students. This book will show you how.

How to Use this Book

Use this book to integrate the Internet into your regular curriculum in fun and engaging ways. Each lesson is ready for immediate use in the classroom with little extra preparation needed. Included are lessons in language arts, social studies, science, mathematics, and art.

Every effort has been made to make this book easy to use. Here is how it is organized:

- Introduction—Describes how to use this book in the classroom, includes suggestions for lesson delivery and describes the hardware and software needed for the activities in this book.

- Teacher Section—Provides the background information necessary to implement the student activities in this book, describes teacher resources available on the Internet, and provides information on copyright issues, Internet safety, and Acceptable Use Policies.

- Student Activities Section—Included are 14 Internet lessons that will enhance your regular curriculum and teach your students necessary computer skills.

Lesson Features

- While each lesson is written with a specific activity and subject in mind, most lessons in this book make use of graphic organizers that can be used in many different lessons and subjects.
  Note: There are additional blank graphic organizers at the back of this book.

- Because the Internet changes so rapidly and Web sites are often short-lived, the lessons in this book have been designed for use with more than one Web site. Many of the lessons have companion Web sites to use as alternatives. This teacher section also provides simple instructions for finding high-quality alternative sites. Note that the Web site you are looking for may not be defunct —see the section titled *What to Do if a Web Site Address Doesn't Work.*

  Should a Web site become defunct, Teacher Created Materials will work to replace it with a similar one. To find the replacement sites for this book, go to our Web site at

  http://www.teachercreated.com

  Click on **URL Updates,** and enter the number of this book, 3832. This will take you to a page with links to any replacement sites.

Introduction

Lesson Delivery

In general, the lessons in this book are structured so that the teacher demonstrates how to navigate to and use a Web site before the students use their own computers to do the activity. In order to show the students what is happening on the teacher's computer screen, a computer projector and a large screen are ideal. (Ask your school technology coordinator if your school has such resources.) Alternatively, the teacher can have small groups of students gather around the teacher's computer screen while the rest of the class is occupied with another activity. If a computer lab is available, you may choose to have most students use an academic skills software program while you are demonstrating the activity to small groups of students. **Note:** Some computer labs are set up so the central computer display will appear on the students' computer screens. If this is the case, you will be able to demonstrate the lesson steps to students while they sit and watch at their own computers.

Limited Computer Access

If computer access is limited or if the students are inexperienced at using computers, you may decide to have students work in pairs. If computer access is limited to one or two classroom computers, many of the activities in this book can first be demonstrated to small groups of students, and then made into a computer center activity for students to complete individually or in pairs as class time allows.

Hardware and Software Needed

Hardware

1. PC/Macintosh computer

2. A modem

Software

1. E-mail software such as *Microsoft Outlook*

2. Internet browser software such as *Microsoft Internet Explorer* or *Netscape Communicator* (**Note:** If you are using *Netscape Communicator*, you will not need a separate e-mail software program.)

3. Internet access from an Internet Service Provider (ISP) such as *America Online* or *EarthLink*

Also recommended is a projection system that will project and enlarge what is on your computer screen for class demonstrations and viewing (ask your school technology coordinator if such resources are available).

Teacher Section

Basic Internet Terms

These basic Internet terms will help you get started:

E-mail—short for electronic mail, which is a typed message sent over the Internet. E-mail is usually a component part of the Internet service provided by companies such as *America Online* or *EarthLink*.

Hypertext and Hyperlink—Text or graphics that, when clicked, take the user to another Web page, Web site, or different part of the same page. This is an example of hypertext: **Home Page**

Home Page—The main or introductory page of a Web site. It is often the first page viewed when visiting a Web site.

Internet—A worldwide network of smaller computer networks which offers data and information sharing, e-mail communication, online commerce, and online activities.

Internet Browser—The software program that allows computer users to view Web sites. The two most common browsers are *Microsoft Internet Explorer* and *Netscape Navigator*.

Log On/Log Off—To connect to or disconnect from an Internet Service Provider or computer network.

Online—Connected to a computer network. It usually refers to being on the Internet.

URL—Uniform Resource Locator, or more simply, a Web site address. Example: **http://teachercreated.com**.

Web Site—A hypertext document on the Internet comprised of one or more Web pages.

World Wide Web (The Web, WWW)—The part of the Internet most used today that is composed of millions of hypertext documents that are easily accessible with Internet browsers such as *Microsoft Internet Explorer*.

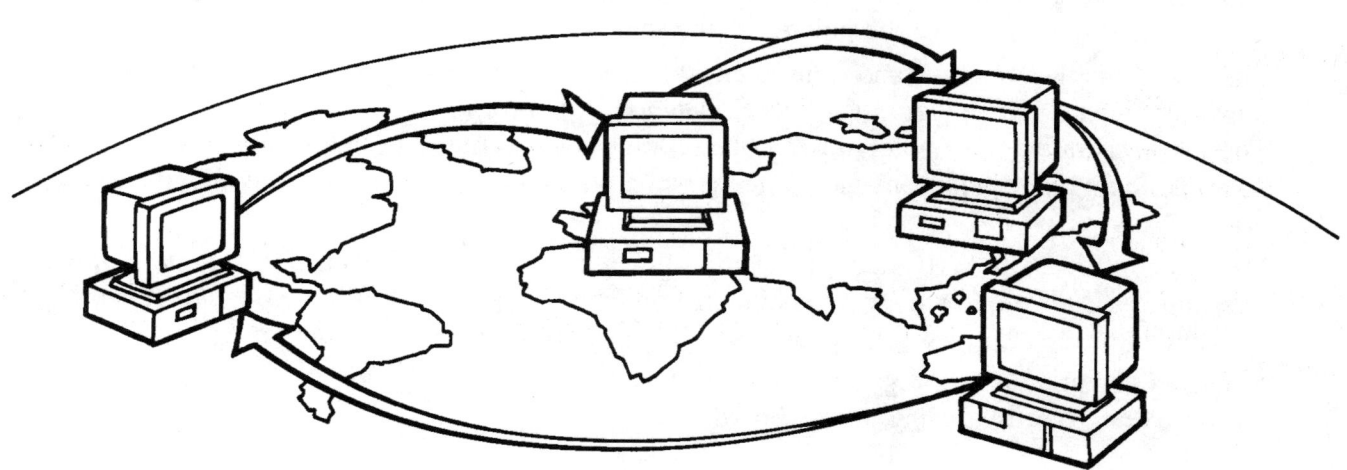

Preparing Students (and the Teacher!) for the Activities in this Book

The activities in this book assume students will have basic computer skills such as:

- moving the pointer around the computer screen
- pointing and clicking
- selecting hyperlinks and hypertext (buttons and words on Web sites that take the viewer to another Web page or another part of a Web page. This is an example of hypertext: **Home Page**
- typing basic text using the keyboard

Other skills that are not necessary, but will save the teacher some time, are the following:

- turning on the computer
- logging on to the computer or network
- logging on to the Internet
- launching an Internet browser such as *Microsoft Internet Explorer* or *Netscape Navigator*

If students do not possess these latter skills, the teacher can perform these tasks for students in advance of the lesson. Or, consider pairing students who feel comfortable at the computer with students who need some assistance. For your convenience, brief instruction is provided below for the skills students will need to complete this book's activities.

Using the Mouse and Keyboard

Most of your students probably feel comfortable using a mouse. For first-time users, the following are suggestions for teaching them:

- With small groups of students, demonstrate how the mouse moves the pointer around the screen. Explain to students that the mouse pad is like the computer screen: wherever the mouse moves on the mouse pad, it will move the pointer on the screen.
- Show students the left-click and right-click (if applicable) buttons on the mouse. Explain that they only need to use the left-click button. Demonstrate how to click on an object to select it. Then demonstrate how double-clicking opens programs and files. To help students get the feel for double-clicking, say "Pizza, pizza!" quickly while clicking the mouse, and then allow students to practice this.
- Using a child-friendly Web site with easy-to-click buttons or words (refer to the *Site to Behold!* Lesson for a Web site to use), demonstrate how to select hyperlinks. Allow your students time to navigate to different pages. Challenge them to return to the Web site's home page.
- Using a word processing program or a Web site, show your students how to position the pointer in a text box and type text using the keyboard.

Logging on to a Computer or Network

Generally, a username and password will be required to log on to a computer or network. Your school district has probably assigned each teacher a username and has asked each teacher to establish a password. There may be a generic username that students can enter when using the computer or network. Consult with your technology coordinator for more specific instructions on how to log on to school district computers and the district network.

Logging on to the Internet

This process varies depending on the Internet Service Provider (ISP) and the type of Internet connection at your school. Many schools have a live Internet connection that does not require users to log on to the Internet. Consult with your technology coordinator for more specific instructions for logging on to the Internet.

Launching an Internet Browser

An Internet browser is the software application that allows you to view and navigate to Web sites on the Internet. Most schools use as their Internet browser either *Microsoft Internet Explorer* or *Netscape Communicator*.

Microsoft Internet Explorer

Netscape Communicator

Once an Internet connection is established, simply double-click the Internet browser icon to launch the program. PC users will most likely find this icon on the desktop. Mac users will most likely find this icon inside the program folder.

Another way for PC users to launch the program is to click on the taskbar at the bottom of the screen, click **Start**, then **Programs**, and then the name of the Internet browser.

Entering a Web Site Address

At the top of your Internet browser is an Address box where Web site addresses are entered.

To enter a new Web site address, highlight the existing address, type the new one, and then press the **<Enter>** key (PC users) or **<Return>** key (Macintosh users) on your keyboard.

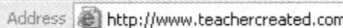

A URL is a Web site address. For example, the URL for the Teacher Created Materials Web site is **http://www.teachercreated.com**.

Typing this URL in the Address box at the top of your Internet browser and then pressing the **<Enter>** key on your keyboard will take you to the Teacher Created Materials Web site. **Note:** It is not always necessary to type the "http://" part of a URL when entering a URL in the Address box of your Internet browser. It is often sufficient to type the rest of the address without the "http://."

You'll Know a Web Site Address Isn't Working When...

- It is taking an extra long time to load the page.

- You receive an error page instead of the page you are looking for.

What to Do if a Web Site Address Doesn't Work

- Check to make sure you typed the address EXACTLY as it appears, with all the characters (such as _, ~, //, etc.).

- Click the **Refresh** button at the top of your screen

- Enter the address again

- Type only the address of the home page and navigate from there. For example, if the address **http://www.nps.gov/parks.html**

doesn't work, try truncating it to become: **http://www.nps.gov**

Then, click the links on the home page to find the specific Web page you are looking for. In some cases, the Web site will have a search engine in which you can type a keyword and find what you are looking for.

Note: Web sites and Web pages are different things. A Web site usually consists of multiple Web pages, with a home page and several pages linked to the home page viewable by clicking buttons on the home page. A Web page is a single page, such as a home page or a linked page.

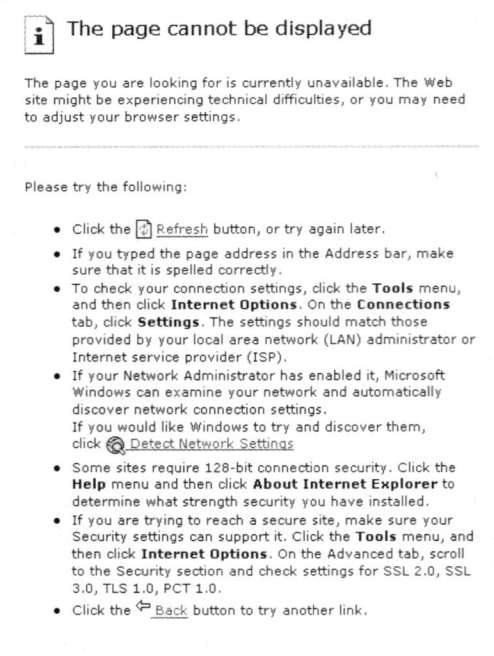

Navigating the Web

Your Internet Browser

As stated above, an Internet browser is a software program that allows you to surf the Internet. Below are pictures of the *Microsoft Internet Explorer* browser and the *Netscape Communicator* browser. Looking at the buttons in the picture as a reference, the following is a description of what each button does:

Back—Returns you to the previous Web page.

Forward—Moves you to the next Web page (if you have already used the Back button).

Stop—Halts the loading of a Web page. This is a handy button if the Web page is taking an extra-long time to load. The delay usually indicates a problem with the Web page, and it's best to click the Stop button.

Refresh—Reloads the current page.

Home—Returns you to the first Web page you viewed when launching your Internet browser.

Search—Brings up a search engine for finding Web sites.

Favorites—Brings up a list of your bookmarks (see the Bookmarking Web sites section for an explanation of bookmarks).

Media—Helps you find movies and music on the Internet.

History—Shows you the Web sites recently visited and allows you to revisit them by simply clicking a hyperlink.

Mail—If you use *Microsoft Outlook* as your e-mail software, you can use this button to access it.

Print—Prints the current Web page.

Edit—Opens *Microsoft Frontpage* or *Notepad* to allow you to edit the current Web page.

Back—Returns you to the previous Web page.

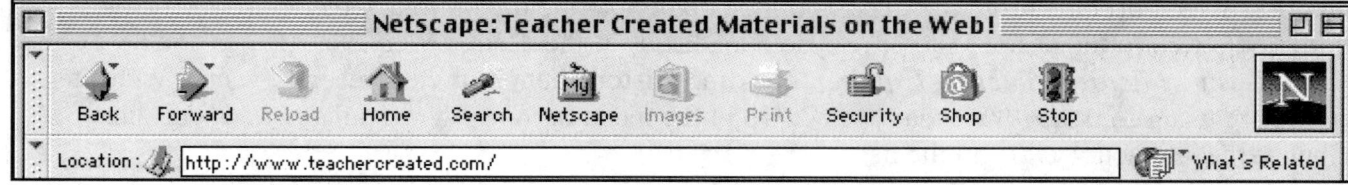

Forward—Moves you to the next Web page (if you have already used the Back button).

Reload—Reloads the current page.

Home—Returns you to the first Web page you viewed when launching your Internet browser.

Search—Brings up a search engine for finding Web sites.

Netscape—Takes you to the *Netscape* start page.

Images—Loads a page's images (if you do not have your Preferences set to automatically load images).

Print—Prints the current Web page.

Security—Displays the security information window.

Shop—Takes you to the Netscape Shopping page.

Stop— Halts the loading of a Web page. This is a handy button if the Web page is taking an extra-long time to load. The delay usually indicates a problem with the Web page, and it's best to click the Stop button.

What's Related—Gives you information about a site you are viewing, such as site ownership, number of links to this site from other sites, and list of sites offering related information.

Hyperlinks

Hyperlinks are buttons, graphics, and text (also known as hypertext) that when clicked, take you to another Web page, Web site, or different part of the same Web page. Examples of hyperlinks are shown below. It is usually very easy to tell that an object or text is hyperlinked. Hyperlinked text is usually colored and underlined and hyperlinked graphics are often outlined or accompanied by hyperlinked text. Another clue that an object or text is hyperlinked is that when you position your pointer over the object or text it takes the form of a hand, indicating that it can be selected. If you select hyperlinked text and then return to the page where you selected it, note that the text is now another color. This indicates that you previously selected the hyperlink.

The following are examples of hyperlinked text (taken from the Teacher Created Materials Web site):

Home Page   Search by grade level, topic or title. View the table of contents of any book, and download sample pages.   **FREE Activities**

Examples of hyperlinked buttons and graphics (from the Teacher Created Materials Web site):

What to Do if You Get Lost on the Internet

It is easy to lose your place on the Internet when you follow one hyperlink after another. If you become lost, either click the Back button at the top of your screen until you return to the desired site or re-type the address of the desired Web site. If you are using *Microsoft Internet Explorer*, click the **History** button to view recently visited Web sites. If you are using *Netscape Navigator*, select **Go** in the menu bar to view recently visited Web sites. Choose the site you want from the list.

Here are some tips to avoid getting lost:

- Use the **Back** button periodically to return to the original Web site. For example, if you leave the original Web site to explore another one, once you are finished exploring the new Web site click the **Back** button until you return to the original site. From there, you can select new hyperlinks, view other Web sites, and then return once again to the original Web site using the **Back** button.
- Open hyperlinks in their own windows. This way you can close the new window and be right back where you started. PC users can right-click on the hyperlink to make a pop-up menu appear. Macintosh users can click and hold the mouse button to make the pop-up menu appear or hold down the Command key as they click on the hyperlink to open the page in a new window.

  For *Internet Explorer*, select **Open in a New Window**. For *Netscape Navigator,* select **New Window with This Link**.

- You can also open a new window before clicking a hyperlink that will take you to another Web site. To do this in *Microsoft Internet Explorer*, click the **File** menu, then choose **New**, and then **Window**. The new window will show you a second copy of the same page. To do this in *Netscape Navigator*, click the **File** menu, choose **New**, and then **Navigator**. The new window will show you your home page. Now you can do your exploring in the new window. Simply click the links you would like to follow without worrying about getting lost. When you want to return to the original Web site, select the old window on the taskbar at the bottom of your screen and the original Web site will be there.

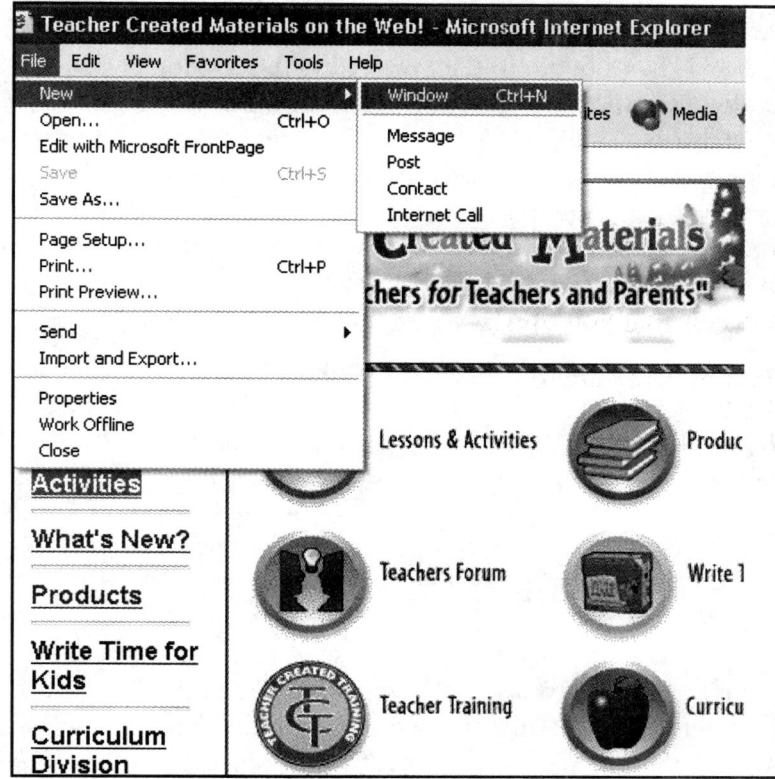

Keeping Students on the Lesson Web Site

Students may be tempted to select hyperlinks that will take them to other Web sites during the lesson. To discourage this, instruct the students to only select the hyperlinks you have demonstrated for them at the beginning of the lesson. If you would like students to be able to visit other sites, teach them how to open a new window to do their exploring (see the tips section under What to do if you get Lost on the Internet).

Using a Search Engine

Search engines allow you to find resources on the Internet based on a word or phrase. Examples of search engines include Google.com, Lycos.com, AltaVista.com, Northern Light.com, and Yahooligans.com (**Note:** Yahooligans.com is a search engine for kids). To practice using a search engine, log on the Internet, launch your Internet browser, and type one of the following addresses in the Address box at the top of your screen: **www.google.com**, **www.lycos.com**, **www.altavista.com**, **www.northernlight.com** or **www.yahooligans.com**. Once the Web site appears, find the Search box.

Position your pointer in the box and click your mouse. Type a word or group of words related to a subject in which you are interested, and then click the Search button or press <**Enter**> on your keyboard.

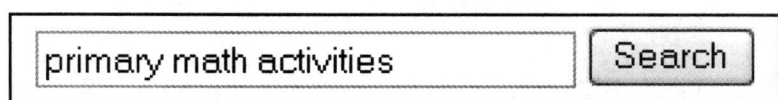

A list of sites related to your subject will appear. Select the hyperlinked text or address (text which is colored) to navigate to the Web site of your choice. Briefly look over the site to see if it is relevant to your subject, then click the **Back** button on your Internet browser to return to the list of sites generated by the search engine. Select a different site, view the site, and return to the list. Try a new search by typing a different word or group of words in the Search box and then clicking the **Search** button or pressing <**Enter**> or <**Return**> on your keyboard. View a few of the sites that appear.

Advanced Searches

An advanced search can help you perform a more specific and efficient search. Advanced searches can be performed using most search engines. To perform an advanced search, from the search page, click **advanced search**. Then decide whether you want the search engine to find ALL of the words you will type, ANY of the words you will type, or an exact phrase that you will type. Type the words, select one of the previous options, and click the **Search** button.

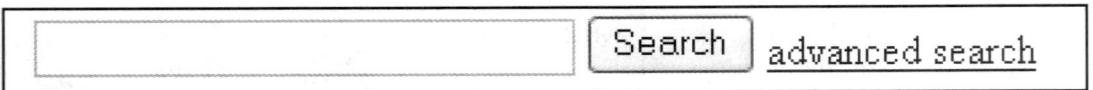

Advanced searches can vary in ease of use and available options. At the time of this book's printing, Google (**http://www.google.com**) was found to be the easiest to use and offered the most options. Northern Light (**http://www.northernlight.com**) allows you to search specific categories of sites such as government Web sites, education Web sites, military Web sites, non-profit Web sites, newspaper Web sites, etc., and allows you to search for Web sites posted between certain dates.

Bookmarking Web Sites

Once you have found a Web site that interests you or is worthwhile for your students, you will want to "save" the site to return to it in the future. "Saving" Web sites is called bookmarking.

- First, navigate to the home page of the Web site that interests you. (**Note:** It is possible only to bookmark specific Web pages, so if you would like access to an entire Web site in the future, it is best to bookmark the home page of the Web site.)

- If you are using *Internet Explorer*, select **Favorites** and then **Add to Favorites**.

- In the **Add Favorite** dialog box, keep or change the name in the **Name** box.

- Choose the folder where you would like the Web site to be saved. If you have not created a folder already, select the **New Folder** button, type a folder name in the **Folder Name** box, and click **OK**.

- In the **Add Favorite** box, confirm that the new folder is selected, and click **OK**.

- To access the Web site you just bookmarked in the future, simply select the Favorites menu, click the folder where you saved the Web site, and then click the Web site. You will jump to the Web site without having to type in the Web site address.

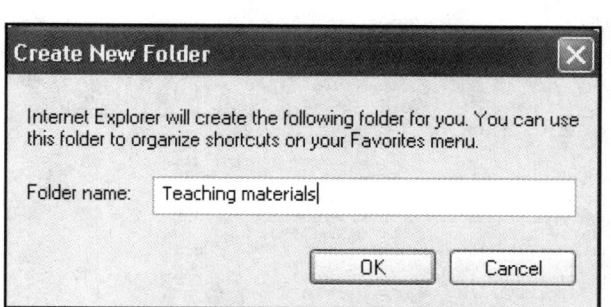

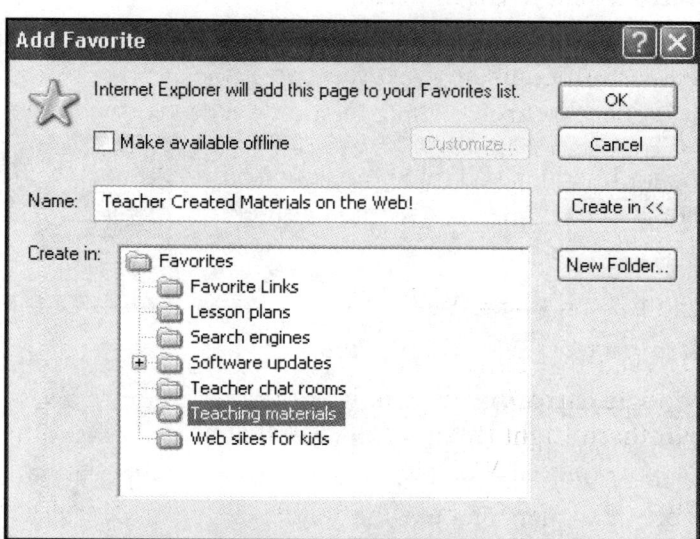

Or, for *Netscape Navigator*:

- Select **Bookmarks** and then **Add Bookmark**.

- If you want to place the bookmark in a folder, rearrange your bookmarks, or add your bookmark to your personal toolbar, go to **Bookmark** and then **Edit Bookmarks**. At this window you can select the name of the bookmark and drag it to a new location.

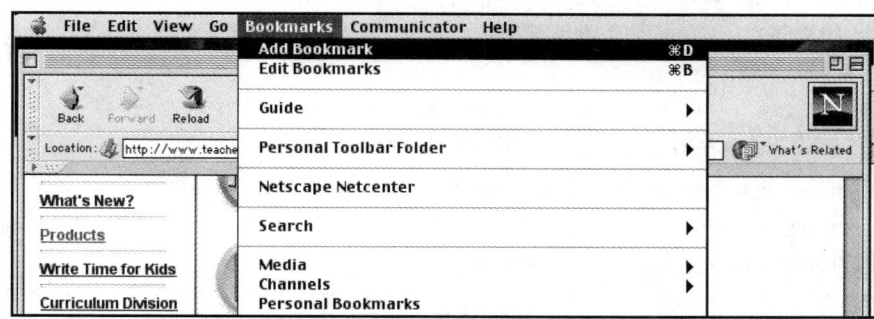

Lesson Plans and Graphic Organizers

There are thousands of lesson plans on the Internet for every grade level and subject. It is easy to find them, print them, and use them in your classroom!

To find them, search one of the following Web sites (active at this book's printing):

Lesson Plans

AskERIC Lesson Plans

http://www.askeric.org/Virtual/Lessons/

Choose a subject, then a topic, and then a lesson based on age level. You can also use the site's search engine to find a lesson plan.

The Lesson Plans Page

http://www.LessonPlansPage.com

LessonPlansPage.com is easy to use with lesson plans organized by subject, grade level, and individual topic. Teachers can use the search engine to find specific lessons. You can also find lessons by choosing a subject, and then a grade level, to see a list of sites organized by specific topic.

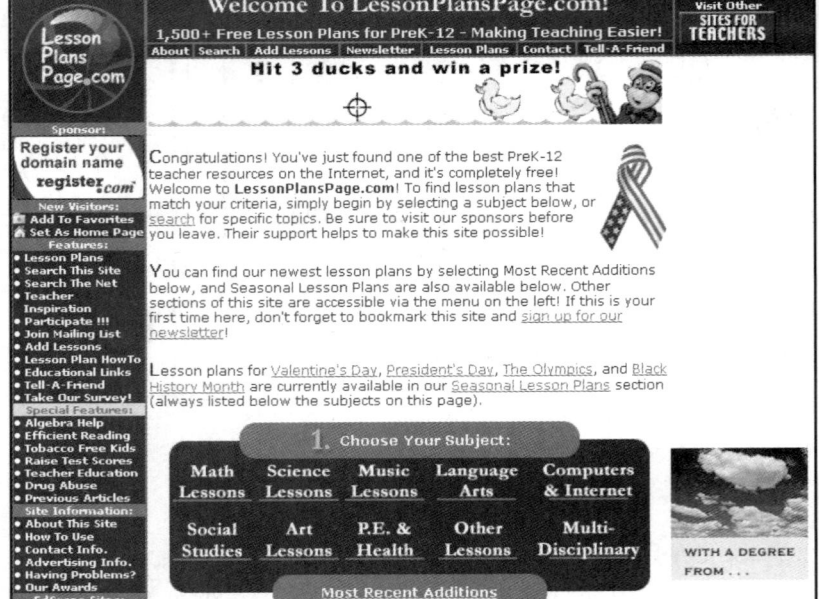

LessonPlanZ.com

http://www.lessonplanz.com/

This site is very easy to search. Simply type the topic in the Search box, choose a grade level, click Search, and your choice of lesson plans will appear.

edHelper.com

http://www.edhelper.com/

This site has lesson plans, worksheets, and puzzles. Many materials are free, but there is a subscription option that gives you access to more materials. To search the site, scroll down to the middle of the page and type a topic in the Search box, or click a category.

Enchanted Learning

http://www.enchantedlearning.com/Home.html

This site does not have a large database of lesson plans, but has information on many topics written for kids, classroom activity ideas, and printouts to use in the classroom on many topics.

Graphic Organizers

Edmonton Public Schools
http://www.angelfire.com/wi/writingprocess/specificgos.html
This site contains hyperlinks to many different graphic organizers. Many come with an explanation for how to use them in the classroom, and others are ready to print.

teachervision.com—Graphic Organizers
http://www.teachervision.com/lesson-plans/lesson-6293.html
There are many ready-to-print graphic organizers on this site.

SCORE
http://www.sdcoe.k12.ca.us/score/actbank/torganiz.htm
Several graphic organizers are shown and explained on this site.

Web Site Reviews—Finding Quality Educational Web sites

At the printing of this book, there are two fabulous sites that evaluate educational Web sites:

EducationWorld
http://www.education-world.com

SBC Pacific Bell Blue Web'n Learning Sites Library
http://www.kn.pacbell.com/wired/bluewebn.

These sites will help you find the best Web sites to use with your students. Both sites organize their reviews by subject and have searchable databases. In addition, both offer e-mail subscriptions that will send you a periodic e-mail with the latest reviewed Web sites. To use one of these sites, simply type the address of the site in your Internet browser address box, press **<Enter>** or **<Return>** on your keyboard, and click the hyperlinks. You can also conduct a search on the site to find a Web site that suits your needs.

Listservs for Teachers

What is a Listserv?

A listserv is an e-mail mailing list of people who share common professional concerns, interests, or personal hobbies. Listservs can be a great way to connect to others who might have valuable advice or insights into what you do everyday as a teacher.

How Listservs Work

E-mails from members of the listserv are sent to everyone else on the list. You can choose to simply read e-mails from others, or you can send e-mails yourself.

A word of caution: depending on how many subscribers there are, and how frequently subscribers send e-mails, you may be inundated with e-mail messages. To counter this, you may decide to join a listserv with fewer members, or if available, request that you receive e-mails in digest format. In digest format you will receive e-mails every so often that contain in a single e-mail the latest subscriber e-mails, instead of receiving each subscriber e-mail in your inbox.

How to Find a Listserv

You can search for listservs by typing *Teacher Listservs* or *Education Listservs* in the Search box of a search engine such as Google. Or, visit one of the sites below (active at this book's printing):

Topica

http://www.liszt.com/

This site has thousands of listservs, and you can find one by using the site's search engine. Type *education* or *teaching* or a word more specific to your interest, and click the Search button to bring up a list of listservs. Click one that interests you to get a description and subscription information.

AskERIC Mailing Lists

http://ericir.syr.edu/Virtual/Listserv_Archives/mailing_list_subscribe.shtml

This site has subscription information and descriptions of about 20 listservs.

Education Listservs

http://www.greece.k12.ny.us/taylor/suny/listservs.htm

This site describes and recommends a few education listservs.

How to Decide which Listserv to Join

Many listservs allow you to look at examples of past discussions. If available, look at past discussions to get an idea if you are interested in joining. In general, though, you can get a sense of whether or not the listserv will be helpful to you by simply reading the listserv description.

How to Join a Listserv

Most listservs simply require you send an e-mail with the word *subscribe* in the body of the message. If you have successfully subscribed, you will receive an e-mail confirmation, followed by messages from the listserv. It is a good idea to save the e-mail confirmation, for usually it contains information on how to unsubscribe to the list. You may want that information in the future.

Teacher Chat Rooms and Discussion Groups

Chat rooms and discussion groups are places of online conversation. They are hosted by any number of Web sites. There are many chat rooms and discussion groups for teachers related to just about any issue in education, such as ESL, special needs, discipline, technology in education, education resources, and on and on. Anyone can join a chat or discussion.

Types of Chats or Discussions

Chat Boards

On chat boards you can view the threads of different conversations and click any one of them to see what a particular person wrote. Click all the threads in one conversation to read the entire conversation. Usually one person posts a question or comment and others respond. To enter the conversation, click a comment thread and then click the response button.

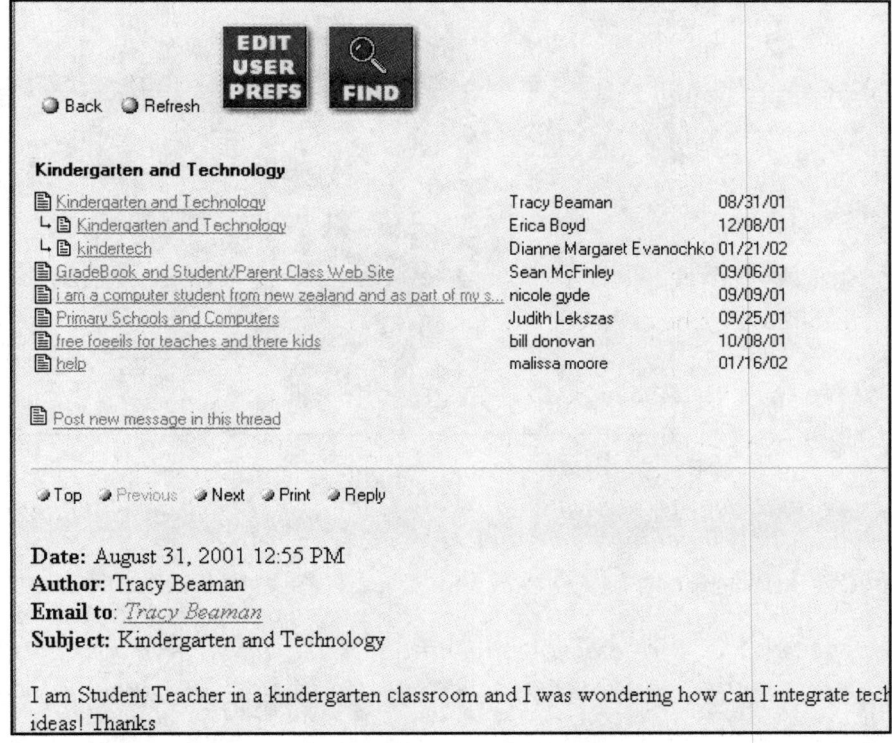

Live Chats

These are scheduled conversations about a certain topic. They often take the format of a question-and-answer session with an expert in the field, of whom you can ask questions directly. They are running dialogues in real time and are usually moderated. To participate in a live chat, go to the hosting Web site at the scheduled time and enter the chat by clicking the appropriate buttons and logging in.

Chat Rooms

Chat rooms are places where people can talk to each other in real time about anything they wish to discuss. Generally the participants set a time to chat and then all log on at that time. The dialogue continually runs until the chat session is over and can be read by everyone. It is just like having a conversation, except you type what you want to say.

Sites that Host Teacher Chats

Teacher Talk

http://www.teaching.com/ttalk/

This site is very simple to use. You must register, but once you do, it is easy to view recent conversations. The search engine is handy for finding information on a particular topic.

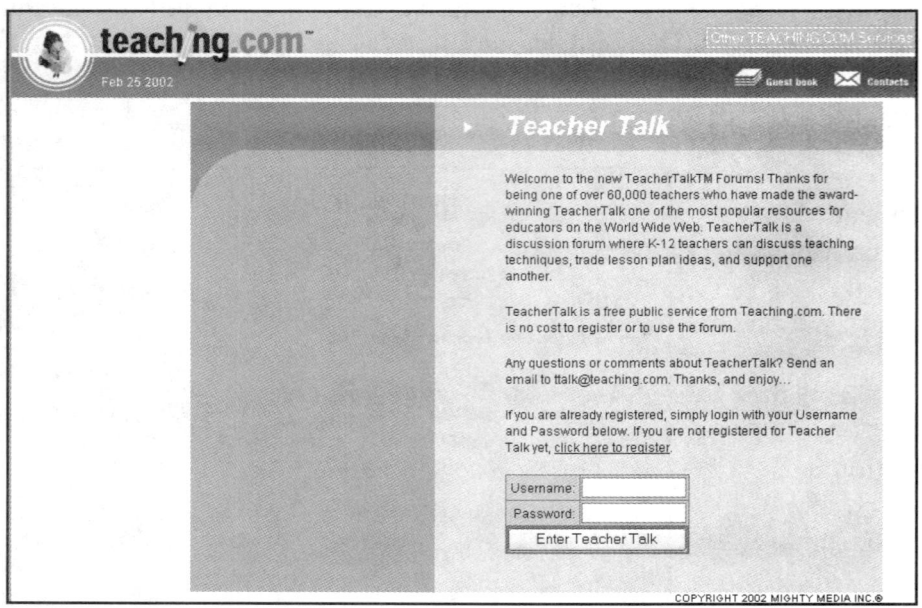

*Teaching.com, the site which hosts Teacher Talk, is owned and operated by the corporate entity **Mighty Media, Inc.** Teaching.com is a free, commercial-free public service for K-12 educators, students, families, media specialists, and administrators. There are over 180,000 educators and students from 88 different countries currently registered as members of Teaching.com. Also note that there are district online services with their own identities and loyal user communities that make up the Teaching.com family of online resources: Teacher Talk (TM), KeyPals Club(TM), EdNow.Com (TM), the IECC, Youth In Action (TM) and Mighty Mentors.*

Teachers.Net

http://teachers.net/

This site hosts chat boards, chat rooms, and live chats. There are grade level chat boards, subject chat boards, beginning teacher, substitute teacher, and regional chat boards. Archives of past live chats are available.

Classroom Connect

http://www.classroom.com/login/landing.jhtml?_requestid=24797

Classroom Connect hosts live chats, student discussions, and teacher discussions about many different topics. An interesting feature is Ask an Expert—you will actually get answers from an expert to questions you pose! **Note:** If you are interested in a teacher chat that has been ongoing, it is most helpful to view the conversation in outline form. You must register at this site as well, but there are many resources in addition to the discussions.

Important Things to Know When Using the Internet

Copyright

Most teachers assume that they can use any Internet material for educational purposes without permission or payment, but this is simply untrue. Anytime you copy and use material from the Internet you run the risk of violating copyright law. Follow these Internet copyright guidelines to ensure that you do not violate the law and run the risk of a lawsuit:

- Be aware that almost everything is copyrighted the moment it is written or created whether it has a copyright notice or not. Examples of copyrighted material include:
  - Digital art (graphics), animations, backgrounds, buttons, bars, headers, and logos
  - Music and sound
  - Games
  - All text
  - Program files
  - Html coding and Java programming
- Do not assume that because it is on the Internet it is in the public domain. However, if a work is in the public domain, you need not worry about copyright. Generally, the public domain includes material published before January 1, 1923, material written by employees of the federal government, and material that the owner has granted to the public domain.
- Copying and distributing material without permission is a violation of copyright law, even if you do not charge anything for the material you distribute. It is best to obtain permission from the owner before distributing material from a Web site. Most Web sites contain a contact e-mail address to which you can write and ask for permission. Most copyright owners are happy to let you use their materials for educational purposes.
- Posting copyrighted information on a Web site without permission is also a violation of copyright law.
- Including the author's/owner's name in a bibliography or footnote WILL NOT protect you from copyright infringement.
- Teach your students respect for copyright. As they quote or copy material from the Internet to use in their presentations and reports, require them to obtain the owner's permission. **Note:** permission is NOT required for factual information, such as, *Americans declared independence from the British on July 4, 1776*. Facts cannot be copyrighted.

E-mail/Chat Netiquette

When writing e-mails, there are common courtesies and tips to keep in mind. Share these tips with your students to help them become more effective and courteous communicators:

- Always proofread your e-mails before sending them to review for grammar and spelling. Also review the tone of the message. Consider how the recipient will interpret it.
- Use mixed case letters; never use all capitals—ALL CAPS APPEAR AS SHOUTING.
- Be brief.
- Include a subject header so the recipient will know the main point of the message before reading it.
- Avoid sending large attachments (over 50k).
- When writing any messages related to your role as a teacher (non-personal messages), always appear professional. Use complete sentences, formal language, and no "emoticons" such as :-).

Internet Safety

Teacher's Role

While the Internet is a wonderful resource for educational information, there are Web sites and chat rooms that contain images and content unacceptable for children. It is important to monitor students' Internet use and follow these safety tips:

- Supervise students while they are online.
- If it is difficult to keep students away from unacceptable sites, consider creating your own list of sites and allowing the students to visit only these sites.
- Monitor e-mail communications. If someone sends you or one of your students an obscene or suggestive e-mail with the intent to harass or threaten, report this to the National Center for Missing and Exploited Children's CyberTipline at 1-800-843-5678 or **www.missingkids.com/cybertip**.
- Use an Internet filtering program or service such as Cyber Patrol, Bess, CYBERsitter, or Safe Net Plus. Note however, that it is not safe to assume a filter will block all inappropriate sites. Supervision is still necessary.
- Note the sites that students are visiting and periodically view them yourself to confirm that they are acceptable.
- Require students to obtain your permission before downloading anything off the Internet.

And in the interest of protecting yourself and your students…

- NEVER send confidential information over the Internet, including information about a student to a parent. Assume that any e-mail you send can be read by anyone on the Internet who has the tools and knowledge to access your e-mail.

Internet Safety Rules for Students

Discuss these Internet Safety Rules with your students, share them with parents, and post them near the classroom computer and in the computer lab:

- Never share your name or your parents' names, your address, your telephone number, and your school name with anyone or on any Web site. If a Web site asks for your first name, give it a pretend name.
- Give out your e-mail address ONLY when your teacher or parent says it's OK.
- Never try to actually meet someone that you have come across on the Internet.
- Never respond to an e-mail message that is mean, has bad words, or says bad things. If someone sends you a bad e-mail, tell your teacher right away.
- Tell your teacher right away if you see something on the Internet that makes you feel uncomfortable.
- Do not click on links in an e-mail sent by someone you do not know.

Acceptable Use Policies

What they are and Why they are Used

With the widening use of the Internet in schools across the globe, there has been a growing concern about the acceptable use of the Internet in the educational setting. Since there is such a variety of materials accessible through e-mail, on the Internet, and the databases that students access, many educational technology experts are suggesting that school districts develop Acceptable Use Policies. Teachers, students, and parents must read and sign these forms before the students are given access to the Internet at their school. Check with your technology coordinator to see if your district has developed an AUP. If a policy has not been developed, visit the site below (which is active at this book's printing) to view some of the many sample AUPs online. Talk to your principal about developing a policy and permission slips for use at your school. Most importantly, make sure that each student who is working online has the following on file:

- A student-signed form of consent to follow district AUP guidelines.
- A parent-signed form stating awareness of the district AUP and releasing the district from responsibility for material that the student may access.
- A student-parent signed form allowing for the release of student work, photographs, or other needed information to be included in collaborative projects, Web pages, or online publication.

On the following pages is the Parent Permission Letter from the Bellingham Pubic Schools, which serves as the district AUP. More information and AUP examples can be found on the following Web site:

http://www.netc.org/tech_plans/aup.html

Internet and Electronic Mail Permission Form

The Bellingham Public Schools

We are pleased to offer students of the Bellingham Public Schools access to the district computer network for electronic mail and the Internet. To gain access to e-mail and the Internet, all students under the age of 18 must obtain parental permission and must sign and return this form to the LIBRARY MEDIA SPECIALIST. Students 18 and over may sign their own forms.

Access to e-mail and the Internet will enable students to explore thousands of libraries, databases, and bulletin boards while exchanging messages with Internet users throughout the world. Families should be warned that some material accessible via the Internet may contain items that are illegal, defamatory, inaccurate or potentially offensive to some people. While our intent is to make Internet access available to further educational goals and objectives, students may find ways to access other materials as well. We believe that the benefits to students from access to the Internet, in the form of information resources and opportunities for collaboration, exceed any disadvantages. But ultimately, parents and guardians of minors are responsible for setting and conveying the standards that their children should follow when using media and information sources. To that end, the Bellingham Public Schools support and respect each family's right to decide whether or not to apply for access.

District Internet and E-Mail Rules

Students are responsible for good behavior on school computer networks just as they are in a classroom or a school hallway. Communications on the network are often public in nature. General school rules for behavior and communications apply.

The network is provided for students to conduct research and communicate with others. Access to network services is given to students who agree to act in a considerate and responsible manner. Parent permission is required. Access is a privilege—not a right. Access entails responsibility.

Individual users of the district computer networks are responsible for their behavior and communications over those networks. It is presumed that users will comply with district standards and will honor the agreements they have signed. Beyond the clarification of such standards, the district is not responsible for restricting, monitoring or controlling the communications of individuals utilizing the network.

Network storage areas may be treated like school lockers. Network administrators may review files and communications to maintain system integrity and insure that users are using the system responsibly. Users should not expect that files stored on district servers will always be private.

Within reason, freedom of speech and access to information will be honored. During school, teachers of younger students will guide them toward appropriate materials. Outside of school, families bear the same responsibility for such guidance as they exercise with information sources such as television, telephones, movies, radio and other potentially offensive media.

As outlined in Board policy and procedures on student rights and responsibilities (3200), copies of which are available in school offices, the following are not permitted:

- Sending or displaying offensive messages or pictures
- Using obscene language
- Harassing, insulting or attacking others
- Damaging computers, computer systems or computer networks
- Violating copyright laws
- Using another's password
- Trespassing in another's folders, work or files
- Intentionally wasting limited resources
- Employing the network for commercial purposes

Violations may result in a loss of access as well as other disciplinary or legal action.

- -

User Agreement and Parent Permission Form

As a user of the _____ computer network, I hereby agree to comply with the above stated rules—communicating over the network in a reliable fashion while honoring all relevant laws and restrictions.

Student Signature _____

As the parent or legal guardian of the minor student signing above, I grant permission for my son or daughter to access networked computer services such as electronic mail and the Internet. I understand that individuals and families may be held liable for violations. I understand that some materials on the Internet may be objectionable, but I accept responsibility for guidance of Internet use—setting and conveying standards for my daughter or son to follow when selecting, sharing or exploring information and media.

Parent Signature _____ Date _____

Name of Student _____

School _____ Grade _____

Soc. Sec.#_____ Birth Date _____

Street Address _____ Home Telephone _____

Use the following form to gain parental permission to display student work on the Internet:

Release to Display Student Work on the Internet

Teacher: _____

School: _____

Dear Parent or Guardian,

During the course of the school year, our class will be publishing student work on the Internet. Anyone with Internet access will be able to view the work we publish. This is an exciting chance to extend our audience, work with partner classes around the globe, and communicate with other "netizens."

By checking the appropriate boxes below, you give or do not give your permission for your child's work and photograph to be published on the Internet. We are all concerned with the privacy and safety of our students. Because of this, we will honor any and all limitations that you may place on this consent to publish.

Please check the appropriate box(es) below:

❑ My child's work, in whatever format, may be displayed on the Internet. His/her first name only may be included.

❑ My child's work, in whatever format, may be displayed on the Internet. Do not include his/her first name.

❑ Photographs of my child may be displayed on the Internet. His/her first name only may be included.

❑ Photographs of my child may be displayed on the Internet. Do not include his/her first name.

❑ My child's work and photograph MAY NOT be displayed on the Internet.

I, _____, give/do not give the above teacher and school permission to display _____'s work on the Internet. If I have given my permission by checking the relevant boxes above to allow my child's work to be displayed on the Internet, I understand the school and district Acceptable Use Policies and release the above teacher and school from any liability resulting from or connected with the publication of my child's work.

Parent or Guardian Signature _____ Date_____

Sample Computer Rules and Restrictions

Discuss and post these rules for general computer usage:

Computer Rules

 • **Wash hands before using the computers**

 • **No food or drink near computers**

 • **Close all programs when finished**

 • **Push in chair when finished**

 • **Do ONLY the activities the teacher has assigned or approved**

Student Activities Section

This section contains 16 Internet lessons to use in your classroom or computer lab.

 **Web Quests**

Direct students to Web sites related to a topic you are currently studying by creating a Web quest. Web quests can be as simple as posting hyperlinks on a Web page that you want students to view, or they can be open-ended inquiries involving several complex tasks. To view examples of the latter, see one of the following Web sites (active at the time of this book's printing):

Come Fly with Me

http://www.murarriess.qld.edu.au/webquests/planequest/index.htm

Animal Hide and Seek

http://projects.edtech.sandi.net/brooklyn/camouflage/

Penguins

http://coe.west.asu.edu/students/phanover/penguin_student_page.htm

Batquest

http://projects.edtech.sandi.net/chavez/batquest/batquest.html

It is simple to set up a Web quest on a topic of your choice. Simply follow the steps below:

Step 1: Locate Worthwhile Web Sites

Whatever your topic, it is usually easy to find high-quality educational Web sites for children that will provide interesting information. Use one of the resources recommended in the Web Site Reviews paragraph of this book to locate high-quality sites, or use a search engine. (**Note:** For maximum efficiency, use a search engine tailored for kids, such as Yahooligans.com.) Remember to choose age-appropriate sites for your Web quest.

Tip: Whenever you are surfing the Web, if you come across a high-quality site that might work for a future Web quest, bookmark it. Then later when you are building a Web quest, you will have at your disposal a collection of high-quality sites from which to choose.

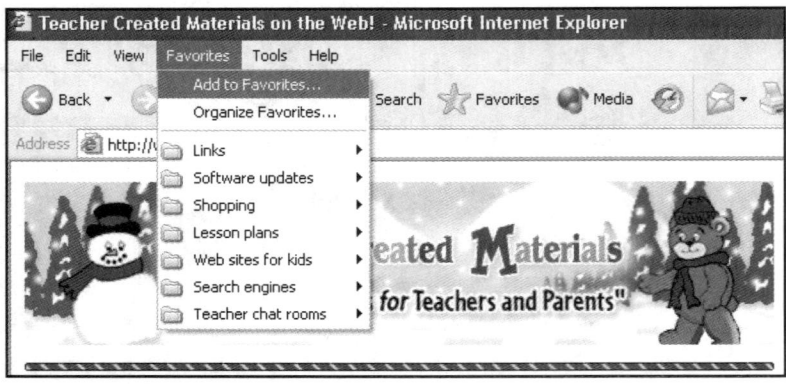

 # Web Quests *(cont.)*

Step 2: Design the Web Quest

The more complex inquiry-based Web quests use the following format: Introduction, Task, Process, Evaluation, and Conclusion. As an alternative, create a Web quest that simply directs students to worthwhile Web sites and asks them to complete tasks using the Web sites. See the Butterflies Web Quest below as an example of the simpler type of Web quest.

Step 3: Create the Web Quest Web Page

The following easy-to-use Web sites (active at the time of this book's printing) allow teachers to post hyperlinks for students to access, and they are free of charge to both the teacher and student:

eBoard

http://www2.eboard.com/eboard/servlevt/IndexLoginServlet

This site offers an easier-to-create eBoard that allows teachers to post information (including pictures and files) for parents and students without creating an entire Web page. Teachers can post assignments, schedules, pictures from field trips, permission slips, announcements, and links to Web sites. Beginning in March 2002, you will need to pay a $29 per year fee to use the service. To create an eBoard, click on Create an eBoard on the left-hand side of the page and follow the directions. The following is an example eBoard, written for a higher grade level. The first picture is the "corkboard" where messages are posted, and the second picture is the full view of the blue note posted on the corkboard. It shows you how you might list hyperlinks for students to access:

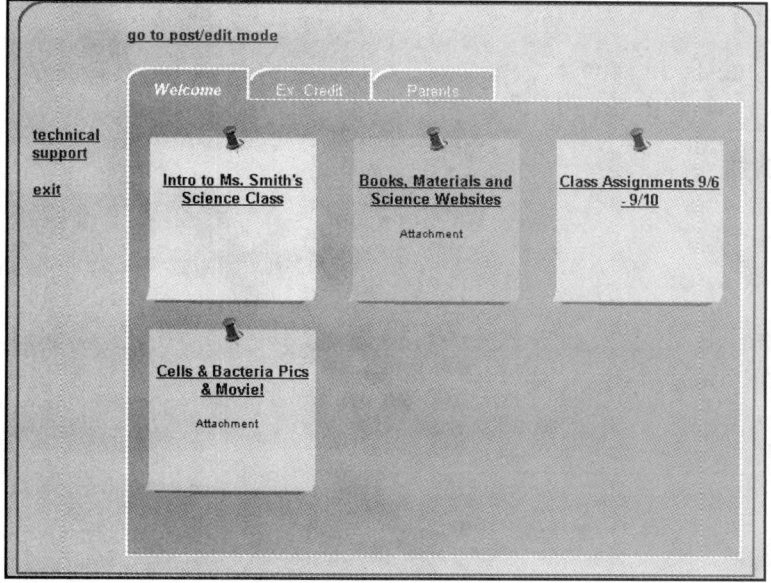

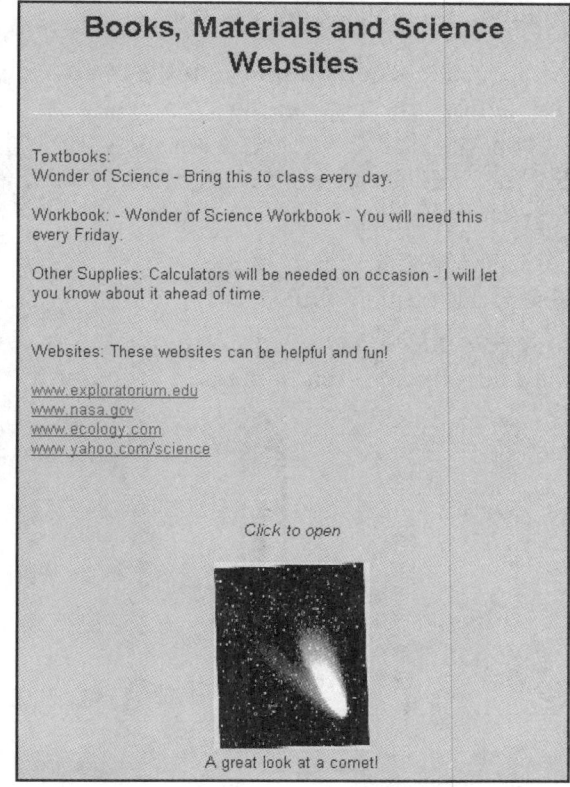

 # Web Quests *(cont.)*

TeacherWeb

http://teacherweb.com

This site is probably the easiest to use for creating Web quests. The sample pages are very helpful. You will need to sign up to use their services. To create a Web quest, from the home page select *Teachers Create your Web!* and then select *Create a TeacherWebQuest.*

Eschoolhouse

http://www.eschoolhouse.com

This site requires you to sign up, but once you do, there are a host of Internet resources at your fingertips, including a free classroom Web page, a collection of searchable Web sites by subject and student age, virtual field trips, games, and professional resources for the teacher. To create a Web page on this site, click *Become a Member,* sign up, and then click *Web Pages.* Then follow the directions to create a Web page.

Step 4: Create a Student Handout (Optional)

Younger primary students will be most successful with a handout that they can follow while viewing the Web sites. See the Butterflies Web Quest handout as an example. Alternatively, you may choose to put more directions on the Web page itself.

Step 4: Embark on the Quest!

Write the URL of the Web page you have created on the board. Explain to the students that they will be using Web sites to learn about the topic you are studying. Distribute and go over the student handout, then allow the students to access the Web page you have created and begin the assignment.

As students become more familiar with Web Quests and the Internet, you can begin to put more instructions directly on the Web page you have created. In addition, you may consider allowing students to do Web quests as homework assignments. However, if you assign a Web quest or any other Internet project as homework, make sure that all of the students can obtain Internet access after the school day ends.

Use Existing Web Quests

Many teachers leave their Web quests posted on the Internet for months and even years. A quick search may turn up an already-created Web quest that you can use with your students.

Example Butterflies Web Quest Web Page

 **Butterflies Web Quest**

Use the Web sites below and the Butterfly Web Quest handout to learn about butterflies:

Web site 1: Zoom Butterflies

What is a butterfly and which are the largest?

http://www.zoomdinosaurs.com/subjects/butterfly/

Web Site 2: BillyBear4Kids.com

The life of a butterfly.

http://www.billybear4kids.com/butterfly/flutter-fun.html

Web Site 3: Beal Butterfly Page—Butterfly Info

The parts of a butterfly.

http://www.ci.shrewsbury.ma.us/Sps/Schools/Beal/Curriculum/butterfly/butterflyinfo.htm

Web Site 4: Beal Butterfly Page—Butterfly or Moth?

How butterflies and moths are different.

http://www.ci.shrewsbury.ma.us/Sps/Schools/Beal/Curriculum/butterfly/mothorbutterfly.html

Butterflies Web Quest
Example Handout

Web site 1: Zoom Butterflies

1. Click on **What is a Butterfly?**

2. Fill in the blank:

   Butterflies are beautiful, flying _____ with large scaly wings.

3. Click on **Extremes: Biggest, Smallest...**

4. Fill in the blanks:

   The largest butterfly in the world is the female _____ _____ _____ butterfly.

Web site 2: BillyBear4Kids.com

1. Draw the life of a monarch butterfly:

2. Fill in the blank:

   A monarch butterfly is black and _____.

 # Butterflies Web Quest *(cont.)*

Web site 3: Beal Butterfly Page: Butterfly Info

1. Label the parts of a butterfly:

Web Site 4: Beal Butterfly Page: Moth or Butterfly?

Butterflies and moths are different. Fill in the blanks to tell how they are different.

1. A moth has feathery or thin antennae, but a butterfly has _____ antennae.

2. A moth has a plump, fuzzy body, but a butterfly has a _____ body.

3. Moths are active at night. Butterflies fly during the _____ .

An Internet Scavenger Hunt

Similar to a Web quest is an Internet scavenger hunt. A scavenger hunt is a series of questions about a topic that the students must use a search engine to answer. You can one of the Web sites listed in the Web quest activity to create a scavenger hunt. Simply post questions to be answered and directions for using a particular search engine on a Web page. Alternatively, scavenger hunt directions can be distributed to the students on paper.

State Symbols

Lesson Summary

Help build students' U.S. geography skills while they learn to use a search engine.

Internet Site

Yahooligans

http://www.yahooligans.com

Companion Site

Ask Jeeves for Kids

http://www.ajkids.com

Preparation

- Copy the *State Symbols* page
- Have available crayons or colored pencils

Lesson Steps

1. Explain to the students that today they will learn how to find information on the Internet. Write the words *search engine* on the board and inform them that a search engine is a Web site that helps people find what they are looking for.

2. While students are watching, log on to the Internet and launch the Internet browser. Remind the students how to enter a URL in the Address box and press the **<Enter>** or **<Return>** key to navigate to the Web site.

3. Point out the Search box on the Web site. Explain to the students that typing a word or group of words in this box and clicking the Search button will pull up a list of Web sites related the words typed.

4. Distribute the *State Symbols* page. Explain that the students will be finding the state flower and animal for three states: New York, California, and a state of their choice. They will also be drawing the state flag for each state.

5. Ask the students for ideas of what to type in the Search box to find the state symbols of New York. Typing *New York State* should work. Write the words on the board.

6. Demonstrate for the students how to type the words *New York State* in the Search box, then click the Search button.

👓 An Internet Scavenger Hunt *(cont.)*

7. A list of sites will appear. Discuss which site the students should choose, and select the hyperlink for that site. **Note:** If you do not find an appropriate site, try the other search engine listed above.

8. Scroll down the page to find the New York state flower, and then instruct the students to fill in the state flower blank on the *State Symbols* page. Use the same site to find the state animal and state flag of New York, or click the Back button on your browser to return to the list of sites found by the search engine. View different sites until you find the information, using the Back button to return to the list of sites when necessary. Allow the students to use crayons or colored pencils to draw the New York state flag.

9. Decide as a class on a third state to research.

10. Discuss the keywords the students should enter for the other two states. Write these on the board and instruct the students to write them on their papers.

11. Direct the students to use the search engine to complete the remaining items on the *State Symbols* page.

Extension Ideas

- Create a simple question sheet on anything the class is studying and challenge students to find the answers using a search engine. You can aid them in the search by writing the words they should type in the search engine on the question sheet. Alternatively, you can review the question sheet before beginning the computer activity, decide together which keywords to enter into the search engine, and write them next to each question so they are handy when the students are using the computer.

- Once students have mastered using a search engine, create scavenger hunts about any classroom topic. The following are ideas for scavenger hunts:

  - Find spelling/vocabulary words on children's Web sites by typing the word in the Yahooligans search engine. When a spelling word is found, the student copies the sentence in which it is used. You may also wish to have them write the URL and the name of the site, and note one interesting feature, to expand their awareness of what is on the Internet.

  - Have the children find 5 animals and 5 insects that live in a rainforest, desert, ocean, evergreen forest, etc. by typing words such as, *rainforest animals* or *desert insects* in the search engine. The students can name each animal/insect they find, briefly describe each one in simple sentences or words, and draw a picture of each one.

  - Have a special class number everyday or every week, such as 32. Challenge the students to see how many Web sites contain the number. Students should note how the number is used on the site, the Web site name, and the URL.

An Internet Scavenger Hunt: State Symbols

Keywords: *New York State*

The state flower of New York is: _____

The state animal of New York is: _____

This is what the flag of New York looks like:

```




```

Keywords: _____

The state flower of California is: _____

The state animal of California is: _____

This is what the flag of California looks like:

```




```

State: _____

Keywords: _____

This state's flower: _____

This state's animal: _____

This is what the flag of _____ looks like:

```




```

 # E-pals

Connect your students with other students across the globe via the Internet. E-pals are a terrific way to help your students develop communication skills, writing skills, and understanding of people in different places and cultures. You can also use e-pals to work with other classrooms on collaborative projects, as well as participate in live chats with experts and famous people.

Use one of the sites below to find e-pals for your students:

Epals.com
http://www.epals.com/

Connects classrooms across the world. Find an e-pal for each one of your students or assign pairs to correspond. E-pals.com allows teachers to create e-mail accounts for students that can be filtered to ensure appropriateness of messages. E-pals.com also hosts discussion rooms for children and live chats with famous people, and offers translations and collaborative projects with other classes.

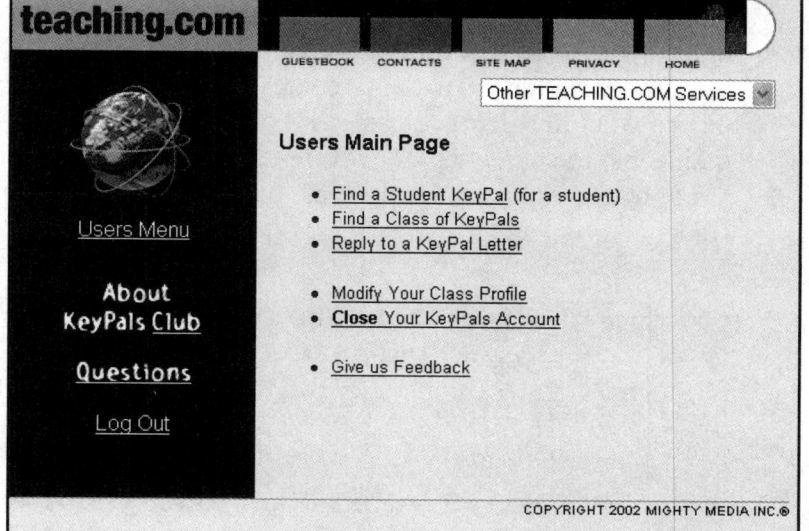

KeyPals Club
http://www.teaching.com/KeyPals/

This site has a huge database of members: 180,000 teachers and students in 88 countries. You will need to sign up, but once you do, it's very easy to find e-pals for your students. KeyPals is one of many services provided free by Teaching.com.

A Girl's World.com
http://www.agirlsworld.com/geri/penpal/index.html

This site for girls ages 7-17 allows girls to choose a pen pal based on interests. The best feature is that no e-mail addresses are given out; the girls write messages to each other on the site itself.

Collaborative project ideas:

- When studying another culture or country, find a class or a student from that country to act as a primary source of information.
- Have students discuss the books they have read over e-mail.
- As a holiday approaches, exchange e-mails about how the holiday is celebrated in another country or even another region of the U.S.; or learn about the different holidays that students celebrate in other countries.

 **E-pals** *(cont.)*

- Join with one or more other classrooms to collect weather data such as daily temperatures, daily or monthly precipitation, or minutes of sunlight each day, and compare the results. Students will learn first-hand how weather can differ in other parts of the country or globe.
- Teach map skills, geography, and time zones by having the students plot their e-pals' locations on a map and determining what time it is in each location.
- Learn about urban vs. rural living by locating e-pals that live in both locations and asking about their daily lives.
- Assign students to e-pals from different countries. Allow them to exchange several e-mails with their e-pals to collect information about their e-pals' daily lives, cultures, traditions, schools, families, vacations, leisure time, etc. Use the template on the next page to allow the students to record what they learn. At the end of the project have students create a report or presentation on their e-pal to share what they have learned with other students. **Note:** For younger students who struggle to write e-mail messages, before each e-mailing session compose a letter on the board for students to type and send to their e-pals. For example,

---

Dear (e-pal's name),

Thank you for your e-mail. I like reading about you.

Today I would like to ask you about your school. What is the name of your school? My school is named (<u>fill in name of school</u>). How many hours a day do you go to school? I go to school (<u>fill in number of hours</u>) hours a day. At my school we have a recess. We get to go outside and play for (<u>fill in number of minutes</u>) minutes each day. Do you have a recess at your school? If you do, how long is it? What do you do during recess?

I can't wait to read your next e-mail.

Sincerely,

(<u>Student's name</u>)

If the students are struggling to read e-mails received from their e-pals, instruct the students to print them, then gather all the students in a circle and read each one out loud. Alternatively, assign pairs of students to compose and read messages together.

All About My E-pal

My e-pal's name is _____.

My e-pal's age is _____ and his/her grade is_____.

My e-pal's school name is _____.

The place where my e-pal lives is _____.

My e-pal has _____ brothers and _____ sisters.

My e-pal goes to school _____ hours per day.

Does my e-pal have a recess?   YES   NO   My e-pal's recess is _____ minutes long.

My e-pal likes to _____ during recess.

My e-pal likes to learn about _____.

My e-pal likes to _____ after school.

My e-pal's favorite book is _____.

Does my e-pal play a sport?   YES   NO   My e-pal plays _____.

Does my e-pal play an instrument?   YES   NO

My e-pal plays the _____.

My e-pal's favorite holiday is _____.

My e-pal's favorite thing about where he or she lives is _____.

My e-pal has taken trips to these places _____.

 A Site to Behold!

Lesson Summary

Use the cards on the following page to direct students to worthwhile activities on the suggested Web site as well as many other worthwhile Web sites.

Internet Site

Boowa & Kwala
http://www.boowakwala.com/

Companion Sites

Funology.com
http://www.funology.com/index.cfm

PBS Kids
http://pbskids.org/fun_and_games/

FunBrain.com Math Baseball
http://www.funbrain.com/math/

Preparation

- Using the suggested Web site, prepare multiple *A Site to Behold!* cards by filling out the top portion and making copies.

Lesson Steps

1. Explain to students that there is a Web site that you would like them to visit using an *A Site to Behold!* card.

2. Show your students an example of an *A Site to Behold!* card with the top portion filled out. Remind them that all Web sites have an address, and show them the Web site name and address on the *A Site to Behold!* card.

3. Log on to the Internet and launch the Internet browser.

4. Briefly review how to enter a URL in the Address box at the top of an Internet browser. Enter the URL on the example card to navigate to the Web site.

5. Read the instructions you have listed next to the first *Go to/Click on:* to your students, and demonstrate these instructions on the Web site.

6. Read the instructions you have listed next to the first *Read or do:*, and then demonstrate these instructions on the Web site.

7. Discuss what the students have learned from the Web site or what they did on the Web site and record one idea on the *A Site to Behold!* card.

8. Read the remaining activities on the *A Site to Behold!* card together.

9. Direct the students to navigate to the Web site and complete the remaining activities on the *A Site to Behold!* card on their own.

 A Site to Behold! *(cont.)*

Extension Ideas

Search for worthwhile Web sites and create a box full of different *A Site to Behold!* cards for students to use at the classroom computer(s). You may decide to laminate the cards and instruct the students to record the things they learned or did in a notebook instead of on the cards.

For an instant computer lab activity, create 10–15 different *A Site to Behold!* cards, make multiple copies of each, and place them in a box. At the computer lab, give one card to each student. Instruct students to complete the activity on the card, including the written portion, turn it in, and then choose a new card from the box. Students should continue to complete different *A Site to Behold!* cards until computer lab time is over.

A Site to Behold!

Name of Web site: PBS Kids

URL: http://www.pbskids.org/fun_and_games

1. Go to/Click on: Joke Machine

   Read or do: learn jokes by other kids

2. Go to/Click on: Coloring Pages

   Read or do: print and color pictures

3. Go to/Click on: Music and Movies

   Read or do: watch movies and listen to songs

Three things you learned or did:

1. I read jokes.
2. I colored pictures of Arthur.
3. I watched a movie from Mr. Rogers about how people make sneakers.

👁 A Site to Behold!

Name of Web site: _____

URL: _____

1. Go to/Click on: _____

   Read or do: _____

2. Go to/Click on: _____

   Read or do: _____

3. Go to/Click on: _____

   Read or do: _____

Three things you learned or did:

1. _____

2. _____

3. _____

👁 A Site to Behold!

Name of Web site: _____

URL: _____

1. Go to/Click on: _____

   Read or do: _____

2. Go to/Click on: _____

   Read or do: _____

3. Go to/Click on: _____

   Read or do: _____

Three things you learned or did:

1. _____

2. _____

3. _____

 # Web Views

Lesson Summary

Students should learn to think critically about Web site content in order to become wise consumers of the Internet. Periodically, direct your students to record their thoughts about the Web sites they visit using the following page titled, *Web Views*.

Internet Site

WWW.4Kids.org
http://www.4kids.org/

Companion Sites

KIDiddles
http://kididdles.com

Funology—The Science of Having Fun!
http://www.funology.com/index.cfm

Kid Safety
http://www.cpsc.gov/kids/kidsafety/index.html

Preparation

- Copy the *Web Views* page
- Locate an example of a "not-so-good" Web site

Lesson Steps

1. Explain to your students that the Internet has many Web sites, some of which are good and some of which are not as good. Today they will practice looking at a few Web sites and deciding if they are good.

2. Discuss what makes a Web site good. Maybe the site has nice pictures, is fun for kids, is educational, or is easy to use.

3. While students are watching, log on to the Internet and launch the Internet browser. Remind the students how to enter a URL in the Address box and press the <Enter> key to navigate to the suggested Web site.

4. View the site together and discuss whether or not it is a good or not-so-good Web site.

5. Show students how to use the *Web Views* page to fill in information about the Web site just viewed. If the class determined that the site is "good," check the box(es) to tell why it is good. If it was determined that the Web site was "not-so-good," determine at least one reason and write that in the appropriate space.

6. View the teacher-selected Web site and discuss whether is it a good or not-so-good Web site.

7. Repeat step 4 to fill in the other *Web Views* box.

Web Views *(cont.)*

Extension Ideas

- Cut the following page in half and keep a stack of *Web Views* next to the classroom computer. Require students to complete at least one journal entry each time they use the Internet.
- Every time students complete *Web Views*, allow them to cut them out and paste them into a notebook. This notebook will become their Internet Journal—a record of the sites they have visited and evaluated.
- Encourage students to bookmark the pages they think are especially worthwhile on the classroom computer.

Name of Web Site: <u>Funology</u>

URL: <u>http://www.funology.com</u>

What I found on this site: <u>I found jokes and recipes. I played games and learned</u>

<u>magic tricks.</u>

This is a GOOD Web site because:	This is a NOT-SO-GOOD Web site because:
☒ It has nice pictures.	_____
☒ It is easy to use.	_____
☒ It is educational.	_____
☒ It is fun.	_____

 Web Views

Name of Web Site: _____

URL: _____

What I found on this site: _____

This is a GOOD Web site because:

❏ It has nice pictures.

❏ It is easy to use.

❏ It is educational.

❏ It is fun.

This is a NOT-SO-GOOD Web site because:

_____

_____

_____

_____

- -

Name of Web Site: _____

URL: _____

What I found on this site: _____

This is a GOOD Web site because:

❏ It has nice pictures.

❏ It is easy to use.

❏ It is educational.

❏ It is fun.

This is a NOT-SO-GOOD Web site because:

_____

_____

_____

_____

 # Authors on the Web

Lesson Summary

After reading a book from the author whose Web site is suggested, direct students to learn about the author by viewing the author's Web site on the Internet.

Internet Site

Mem Fox
http://www.memfox.net/

Companion Site

Jan Brett
http://www.janbrett.com

Preparation

- Have your students read a book by the author whose Web site is suggested.
- List the Web site name and URL on the board that students will access during this lesson.

Lesson Steps

1. Have your students read the book(s) you have chosen. **Note:** This can be the same book for all students, or students may choose their book.

2. Explain to your students that today they will find information on the Internet about the author of the book they just read.

3. While students are watching, log on to the Internet and launch the Internet browser. Remind the students how to enter a URL in the Address box and press the <Enter> key to navigate to the Web site.

4. View the Web site. Click the hyperlinks to explore the different Web pages on the site. Read some of the information about the author together.

5. Explain to your students that they will be using this site to complete an *Authors on the Web* card.

6. Distribute *Authors on the Web* cards and assist the students in completing the first four lines. Read the next three statements on the card together and discuss with the students where they might find this information on the Web site.

7. Direct the students to navigate to the Web site and complete their *Authors on the Web* cards.

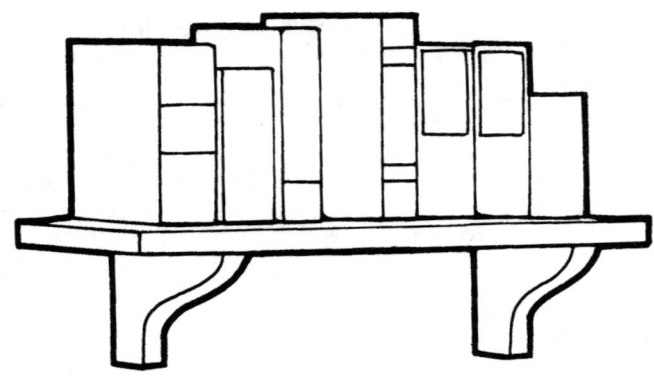

　　　　　　　46　　　　　　　© *Teacher Created Materials, Inc.*

 Authors on the Web *(cont.)*

Extension Ideas

- During the course of the year, allow students to search the Internet for information on authors of books they have read. Allow them to complete an *Authors on the Web* card for every book they read. You might consider giving extra credit for each card completed.

- If you use reading and/or writing portfolios with your class, consider allowing your students to include *Authors on the Web* cards in their portfolios.

- Have students use the *Authors on the Web* cards to prepare reports or projects about authors. You might add questions to the card, such as:

    - "How did the author come up with the idea for the book?"

    - "Where was the author or illustrator born?"

    - "What does the author or illustrator like to do?"

- Create *Illustrators on the Web* cards for students to find information on the illustrators of the books they have read.

Authors on the Web

My book: The Hat

The author's name: Jan Brett

Name of the Web site: Jan Brett.com

URL: http://www.janbrett.com

This is place where my author lives: Massachusetts

Titles of the books my author has written: Hedgie's Surprise, Trouble with Trolls, The Mitten

This is one thing I learned about my author: She liked to read and draw when she was little.

📖 Authors on the Web

My book: _____

The author's name: _____

Name of the Web site: _____

URL: _____

This is place where my author lives: _____

Titles of the books my author has written: _____

This is one thing I learned about my author: _____

📖 Authors on the Web

My book: _____

The author's name: _____

Name of the Web site: _____

URL: _____

This is place where my author lives: _____

Titles of the books my author has written: _____

This is one thing I learned about my author: _____

 # Creating My Own Art

Lesson Summary

Students view several famous paintings, write about their favorite painting, and then create their own work of art.

Internet Site

The Art Institute of Chicago: Art Access
http://www.artic.edu/artaccess/

Companion Site

National Gallery of Art NGA Kids
http://www.nga.gov/kids/

Preparation

- Copy the *Creating My Own Art* page
- Write the Web site name and URL on the board
- Have crayons and colored pencils available

Lesson Steps

1. Explain to your students that many beautiful and famous works of art can be seen on the Internet.

2. While students are watching, log on to the Internet and launch the Internet browser. Remind the students how to enter a URL in the Address box and press the <Enter> key to navigate to the Web site.

3. View several paintings with the students. As you view each painting, point out the name of the painting and the name of the artist. Discuss with the students what is in the picture (i.e., people, buildings, trees, etc.), the different colors the artists used, and what is happening in the scene (or if it is a portrait, what the subject may be thinking or feeling).

4. Distribute a *Creating My Own Art* page to each student. Explain that now they will be viewing the site on their own and choosing a painting that they like the most. Briefly go over the top portion of *Creating My Own Art* page to prepare students to complete the page on their own. Have them write the name of the Web site and the URL on the page. **Note:** You may want the students to fold the page in half so that only the top portion of the page can be seen.

5. Direct the students to navigate to the Web site, view several more paintings, choose a favorite painting, and complete the top portion of the *Creating My Own Art* page.

6. When finished with the top portion of the page, explain to the students that they will now create their own art. Direct them to use crayons or colored pencils to create a "painting" on the bottom portion of the *Creating My Own Art* page.

Creating My Own Art *(cont.)*

Extension Ideas

- Consider allowing students to create a real painting by using larger pieces of paper and paint. The students can prepare for the painting by first drawing a smaller version with crayons or colored pencils on the *Creating My Own Art* page.

- View other types of art on the Web site such as sculpture or pottery and discuss the ways in which they were made. Discuss how art takes many shapes and forms, and ask what types of art the students themselves have made. Explain how art is a way to share thoughts and feelings with other people. Ask students if they have shared their feelings with another person by making art for that person.

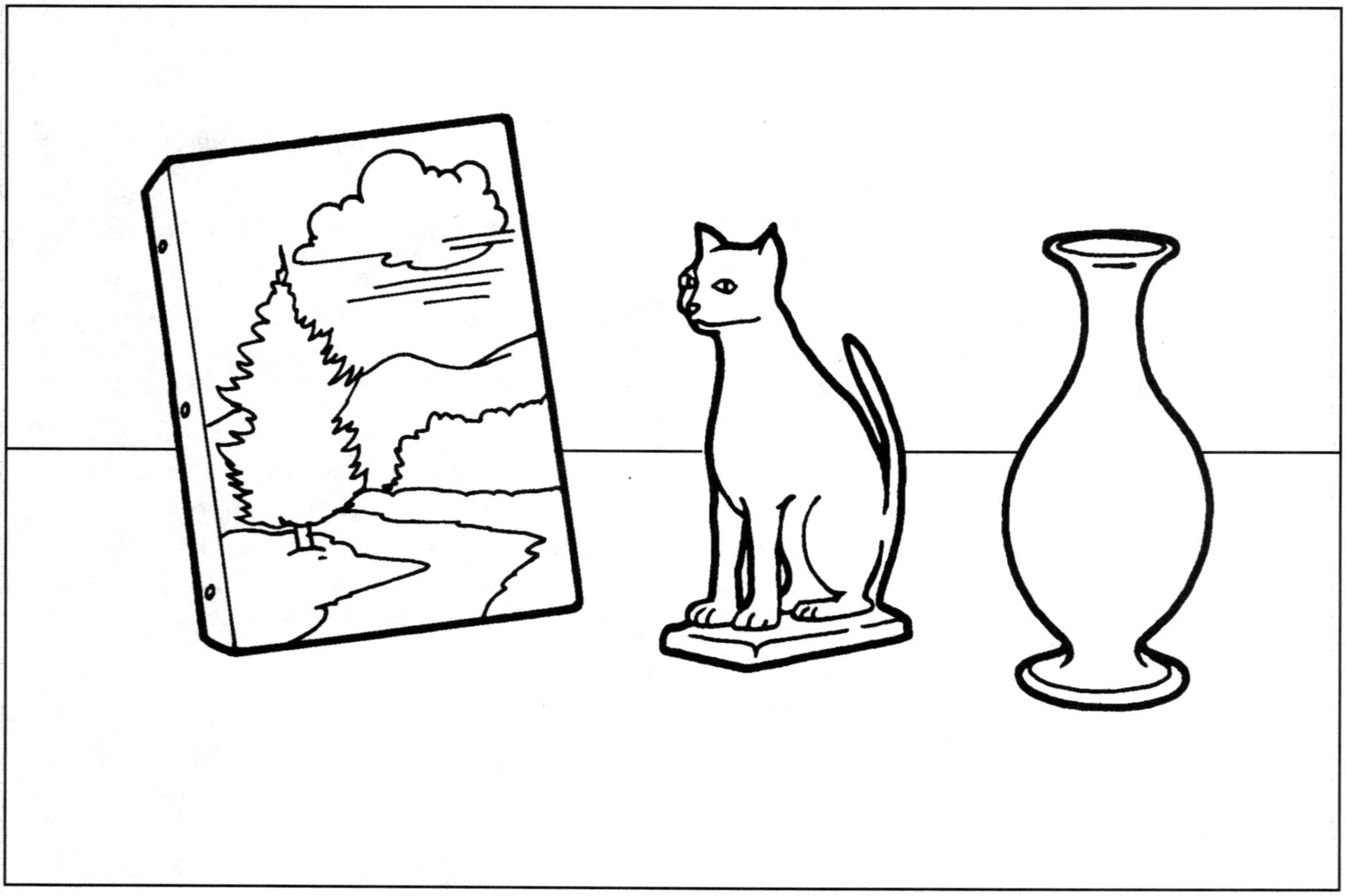

Creating My Own Art

Web site name:_____

URL: _____

The painting I liked best is called: _____

The artist's name is: _____

In the painting, I see these things: _____

I see these colors in the painting: _____

I like this painting because: _____

Here is my own work of art:

Mapping Where I Live

Lesson Summary

The students locate the place where they live using an interactive mapping Web site, and then use the map they found to draw a map of their neighborhood.

Internet Site

MapQuest
http://www.mapquest.com

Preparation

- Make sure that all the students know the address of the place where they live and the nearest cross street
- Have available crayons or colored pencils
- Write the Web site name and URL on the board

Lesson Steps

1. Explain to the students that today they will find a map of where they live on the Internet.

   First however, they will find a map of the neighborhood where the school is located.

2. While students are watching, log on to the Internet and launch the Internet browser. Remind the students how to enter a URL in the Address box and press the **<Enter>** key to navigate to the Web site.

3. Discuss the Web site. Point out the boxes for entering an address. Type the address of the school and click the Search button or press the **<Enter>** key on the keyboard.

4. Discuss the map that appears. Point out where the school is located, the street in front of the school, and the nearest cross street, as well as any other intersections or places of interest to the students. **Note:** If locating their house on a map is too difficult for your students, skip the next few steps and instead have them draw the map of the neighborhood surrounding the school.

5. Explain to the students that they will now find a map of where they live using this Web site. Distribute copies of the *Mapping Where I Live* page. Instruct the students to write their address in the appropriate place at the top of the page.

6. Direct the students to navigate to the Web site, type their addresses, and click the **Search** button or press the **<Enter>** key on the keyboard.

7. When a map appears, challenge students to find where their house or apartment is located. Instruct them to find the nearest cross street to their house or apartment to assist them in finding their house. Provide assistance as necessary.

8. Explain to the students that now they will draw a map of their neighborhood using the map on the Web site. In the box on the *Mapping Where I Live* page, have them draw the map that is on the computer screen. Encourage them to draw their houses on their maps.

 # Mapping Where I Live *(cont.)*

Extension Ideas

- Allow students to experiment with the zoom in and zoom out buttons next to the map. Discuss what is happening: zooming in is like looking through a magnifying glass—you see the map closer up, but you see a smaller part of the neighborhood; zooming out is like taking the magnifying glass away, but now you see more of the neighborhood.

- Brainstorm with the students how people might use this Web site. Why do people need maps? People use maps to get from one place to another, or to find a place. Sometimes people use maps to figure out how long it will take them to get somewhere.

- Use the nearby locations feature to show schools, churches, parks, etc. on the map. Use this feature to confirm that the school is where you think it is!

- On the same Web site, if the feature is available, have them view an aerial satellite image of the neighborhood surrounding the school and then identify the school buildings.

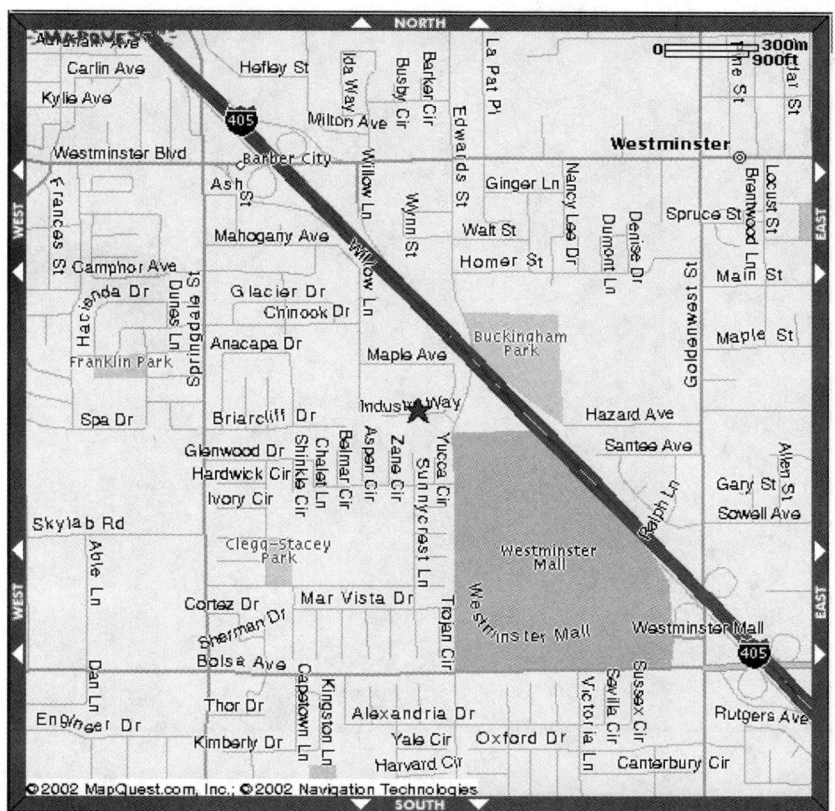

© *mapquest.com*

 # Mapping Where I Live

Web site name:_____

URL: _____

My address: _____

A map of where I live:

```
┌─────────────────────────────────────────────┐
│                                             │
│                                             │
│                                             │
│                                             │
│                                             │
│                                             │
│                                             │
│                                             │
│                                             │
│                                             │
│                                             │
│                                             │
│                                             │
│                                             │
│                                             │
│                                             │
│                                             │
│                                             │
│                                             │
│                                             │
└─────────────────────────────────────────────┘
```

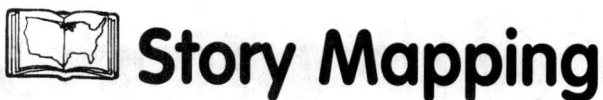 Story Mapping

Lesson Summary

The students read a story on the Internet, then determine the beginning, middle, and end of the story.

Internet Site

Absolutely Whootie: Stories to Grow By
http://hazel.forest.net/whootie/default.html

Preparation

- Write the name of the Web site and its URL on the board
- Copy the *Story Mapping* page
- Locate an appropriate story on the suggested Web site

Lesson Steps

1. Explain to the students that today they will read a story on the Internet.

2. While students are watching, log on to the Internet and launch the Internet browser. Remind the students how to enter a URL in the Address box and press the **<Enter>** key to navigate to the Web site.

3. Show the students how to navigate to the story you have selected.

4. If the students are able to read the story on their own, instruct them to return to their computers, navigate to the Web site, locate the story, and read it on their own. If the students are not able to read the story on their own, read the story as a class.

5. Discuss as a class how every story has a beginning, a middle, and an end. Using an example such as *Little Red Riding Hood*, challenge the students to describe the beginning, middle, and end of a story. Record the beginning, middle, and end of the story on the *Story Mapping* page while the students are watching. Then, discuss what part of the story they liked best and why, and record their response at the bottom of the *Story Mapping* page.

6. Allow students to recall and describe in small groups the Internet story they just read. Or, recall the story as a class.

7. Explain that now they will use the *Story Mapping* page to record the beginning, middle, and end of the story. Distribute the *Story Mapping* pages to the students and direct them to complete the boxes.

8. Now instruct the students to think of which part of the story they liked best and why. Direct them to record their thoughts at the bottom of the page.

Extension Ideas

- Using the *Site to Behold* cards from the Site to Behold lesson, direct the students to worthwhile and reading level-appropriate stories on the Internet. You can create a box of cards for the classroom computer center that direct the students to different stories. Challenge them to complete a *Story Mapping* page for every story they read.

 **Story Mapping**

Story Title:

Author:

Beginning

Middle

End

The part I liked best is_____because_____.

Current Events Online

Lesson Summary

With the teacher's help, the students read a news article on the Internet and decide the *Who, What, Where,* and *When* of the news item.

Internet Site

Yahooligans! News
http://www.yahooligans.com/content/news/

Preparation

- Navigate to the news Web site and locate an appropriate article for your students
- Write the Web site name and URL on the board
- Copy the *Current Events Online* page

Lesson Steps

1. Explain to the students that the Internet is a great place to learn about what is happening in the world. In fact, there are news sites just for children, and they will be looking at one today.

2. While students are watching, log on to the Internet and launch the Internet browser. Remind the students how to enter a URL in the Address box and press the **<Enter>** key to navigate to the Web site.

3. Take a moment to look at the home page and discuss some of the news headlines and features. Then, navigate to the article you have selected.

4. Read the article together.

5. Distribute the *Current Events Online* page and discuss the boxes. Discuss what *Who, What, Where,* and *When* means in terms of a current event. Explain to the students that it is their job to decide the *Who, What, Where,* and *When* of the article.

6. Allow the students a moment to discuss in small groups what they might write in the *Who* box, then discuss it as a class. Complete the *Who* box together. Repeat this process for the *What, Where,* and *When* boxes.

Extension Ideas

- Allow advanced readers to complete a *Current Events Online* page at the classroom computer when they are finished with their regular reading.
- Invite students to imagine what current event they would write about and post on a Web site. Then direct the students complete a *Current Events Online* page about the current event they have chosen.
- Visit the suggested Web site once a week to discuss current events as a class.

Current Events Online

Web site name:

URL:

Who:

What:

Current Event:

Where:

When:

 # Look at What I Know!

Lesson Summary

After learning about dinosaurs online, challenge your students to recall several facts about dinosaurs.

Internet Site

Zoom Dinosaurs.com
http://www.enchantedlearning.com/subjects/dinosaurs/

Preparation

- Write the Web site name and URL on the board
- Copy the *Look at What I Know!* page
- Visit the Web site before the lesson so that you can direct students to learn what you feel is most important

Lesson Steps

1. Explain to the students that today they will be learning about dinosaurs using the Internet.

2. While students are watching, log on to the Internet and launch the Internet browser. Remind the students how to enter a URL in the Address box and press the **<Enter>** key to navigate to the Web site.

3. Read about dinosaurs together. Click the hyperlinks to define words or to learn more about certain aspects of dinosaurs.

4. Distribute the *Look at What I Know!* page to the students. Instruct them to fill in the name of the Web site and the URL at the top of the page. Then discuss how the students will be using the page to record facts about dinosaurs.

5. Allow students a few moments to recall what they learned from the Web site, then brainstorm as a class. Refer to the Web site as necessary. Record ideas on the *Look at what I Know!* page.

Extension Ideas

- Use the *Look at What I Know!* page during every science or social studies unit. Direct students to access a factual Web site related to the unit and record what they have learned from the Web site on the *Look at What I Know!* page.

- At the class computer center, provide copies of the *Look at What I Know!* page for students to complete when they have extra time, or during centers time.

 # Look at What I Know!

Name of the Web Site: _____

URL: _____

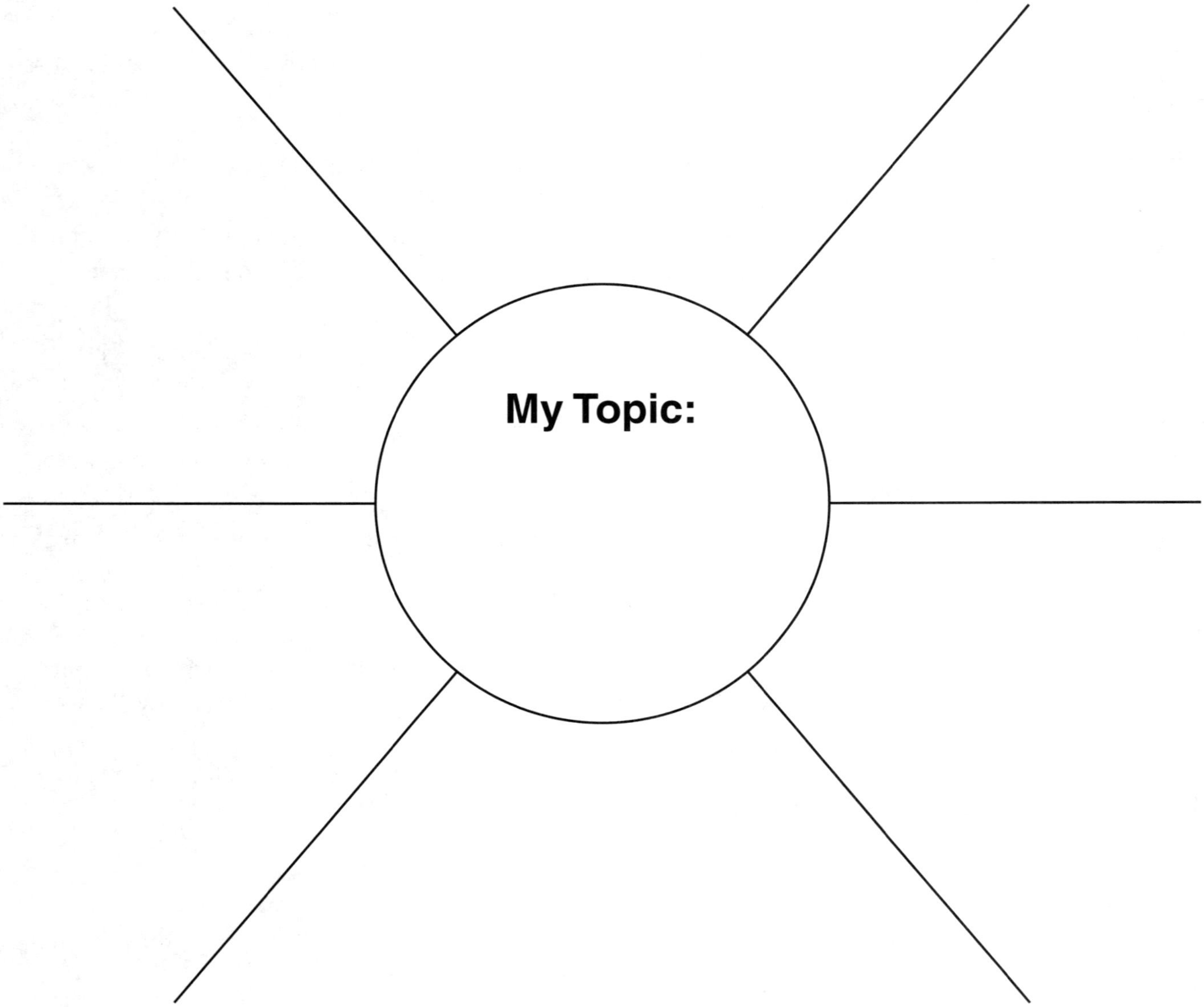

My Topic:

 # Online Words

Lesson Summary

Students use an online dictionary to define their spelling or vocabulary words while building computer skills.

Internet Site

WordCentral.Com
http://www.wordcentral.com/

Companion Site

Little Explorers Picture Dictionary
http://www.enchantedlearning.com/Dictionary.html

Note: For younger children, the companion site is a better choice.

Preparation

- Have students' spelling/vocabulary lists available
- Copy the *Online Words* page
- Write the Web site name and URL on the board

Lesson Steps

1. Explain to the students that today they will use a dictionary on the Internet to find the definitions of their spelling/vocabulary words.

2. Distribute the students' spelling/vocabulary lists and the *Online Words* page. Explain to the students that for each word, they will first write what they think the word means, find what the word actually means and write the definition in their own words, and then compose a sentence using the word.

3. Think of a word and ask students what they think it means. Write the word and the students' prediction on the *Online Words* page. Instruct the students to do the same.

4. While students are watching, log on to the Internet and launch the Internet browser. Remind the students how to enter a URL in the Address box and press the **<Enter>** key to navigate to the Web site.

5. Navigate to the student dictionary by following the appropriate hyperlinks. Point out the box where the students will type each spelling/vocabulary word. Type the example word and click the Find/Search button.

6. When the definition appears, read it out loud. Then, working with the students, come up with another way of defining the word and write that definition below the prediction on the *Online Words* page. Discuss how the prediction was similar or different from the actual meaning.

7. Together compose a sentence for the word and write that on the *Online Words* page.

 # Online Words *(cont.)*

8. Allow the students to use the Internet, their spelling/vocabulary lists, and the *Online Words* page to predict a definition, find a definition, and write a sentence for each word. **Note:** If the definitions offered by the Internet site are written at a reading level that is too difficult for children to decipher on their own, consider having them use the companion site, pairing students, or doing the entire activity as a class.

Extension Ideas

- Anytime the students come across a word they do not know in their reading or daily life, challenge them to predict its definition, and then use the classroom computer to look up the word. Create a *New Words* sheet for students to record new words, their predicted definitions, and their actual definitions. Keep the sheets by the computer. Also, bookmark the dictionary site on the classroom computer and show students how to access it so you do not have to interrupt what you are doing to help them define a word.

- Consider designating one student the Word Hunter—the person who can use the classroom computer to look up words—when the entire class is reading together, or anytime the entire class comes across an unfamiliar word.

- If your students are comfortable doing so, allow them to use a search engine to find their spelling/vocabulary words used in context on other sites. This might help them compose sentences.

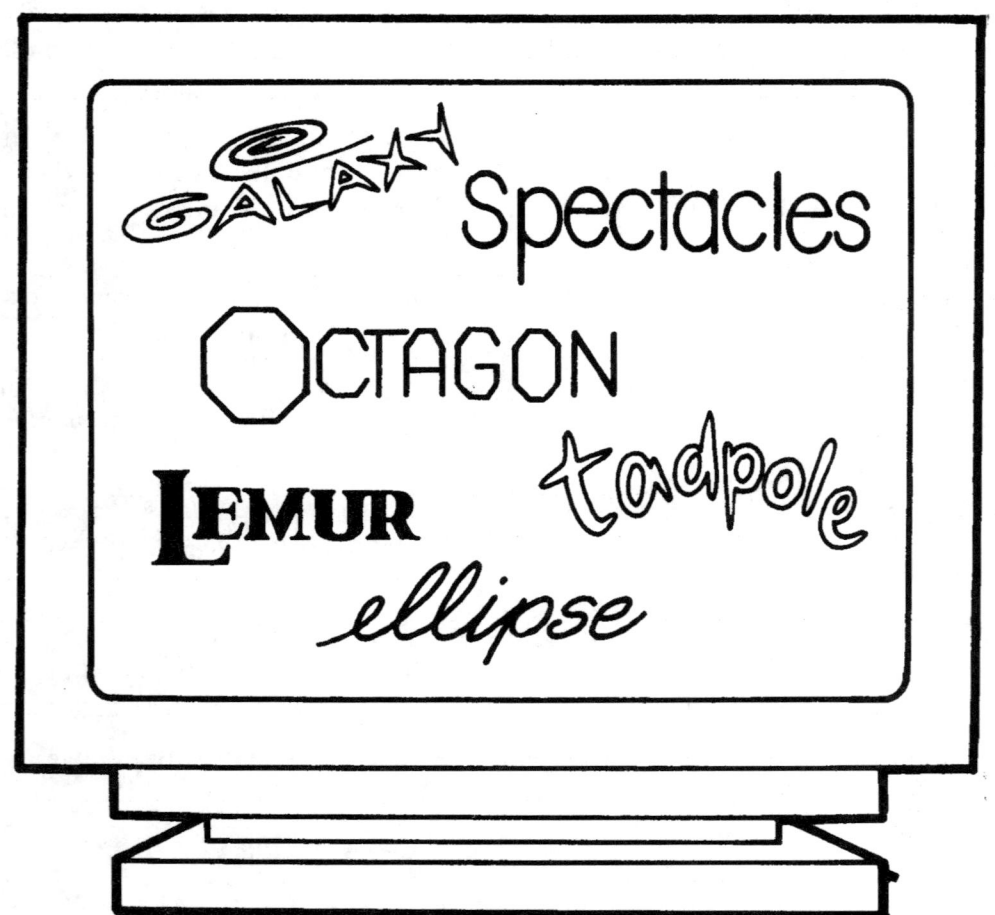

Online Words

Web site name:_____

URL: _____

Word: _____
What I think the word means:_____
What the word means: _____
Sentence: _____

- -

Word: _____
What I think the word means:_____
What the word means: _____
Sentence: _____

- -

Word: _____
What I think the word means:_____
What the word means: _____
Sentence: _____

- -

Word: _____
What I think the word means:_____
What the word means: _____
Sentence: _____

- -

Word: _____
What I think the word means:_____
What the word means: _____
Sentence: _____

- -

Word: _____
What I think the word means:_____
What the word means: _____
Sentence: _____

- -

🇺🇸 The United States of America

Lesson Summary

Help your students brainstorm what they know and want to know about the United States of America, and then use the Internet to learn about the United States.

Internet Site

Ben's Guide for Kids to U.S. Government
http://bensguide.gpo.gov/k-2/index.html

Preparation

- Write the Web site name and URL on the board
- Copy *The United States of America* pages, front to back if possible
- Create a KWL chart on the board similar to the one on the first *The United States of America* page.
- Have available crayons or colored pencils

Lesson Steps

1. Tell the students that today they will learn about the United States of America using the Internet, but first, they will brainstorm what they already know about the United States.

2. Distribute *The United States of America* pages. Then, help the students brainstorm what they already know about the United States. Record the students' ideas in the first column of the chart you created on the board while the students record the same ideas on their pages.

3. Next, ask students what they would like to know about the United States of America and record these questions in the second column of the chart while the students record the questions on their pages.

4. Explain to the students that now they will use the Internet to help answer some of their questions about the United States.

5. While students are watching, log on to the Internet and launch the Internet browser. Remind the students how to enter a URL in the Address box and press the **<Enter>** key to navigate to the Web site.

6. Begin looking for the answers to the students' questions on the suggested Web site. When you find an answer, record it in the *What I Learned* column. Answer at least three of the students' questions using the Web site.

7. Next, direct the students' attention to the second *The United States of America* page. Explain that they will need to complete this page on their own using the Web site. **Note:** Assist younger students as necessary.

8. Direct the students to navigate to the Web site on their own computers and complete the assignment.

The United States of America

Extension Ideas

- Think of more questions that the students can answer using the Web site.
- Have the students use the information on *The United States of America* page to create a book. Each page can contain one fact about the United States and a drawing to go with it. Post the books on a bulletin board and title the board, *Learning About the USA on the Internet*.
- Use the KWL chart to brainstorm prior to learning about any topic. Then find an Internet site that is age-appropriate and create a sheet of questions for students to answer using the site. This will help introduce students to the new topic and motivate them to learn more.

The United States of America

What We **K**now	What We **W**ant to Know	What We **L**earned

The United States of America

The Nation

The United States is on the _____ _____ continent.

On a map, above the United States is the country called _____, and below the United States is a country called _____.

There are _____ states in the United States.

The capital of the United States is _____.

Symbols of the United States

This is a picture of the flag of the United States:

There are _____ stripes and _____ stars on The United States of America's flag.

The national bird of the United States is:_____.

The _____ House (if the home of the President of the United States).

The Statue of Liberty is located in _____ _____.

 **Daily Weather**

Lesson Summary

Students read daily weather information on the Internet and record it in their logs.

Internet Site

The Weather Channel
http://www.weather.com

Preparation

- Write the Web site name and URL on the board
- Copy the *Weather Log* page
- Have available crayons or colored pencils

Lesson Steps

1. Explain to the students that today they will be finding weather information about their city or town using the Internet.

2. While students are watching, log on to the Internet and launch the Internet browser. Remind the students how to enter a URL in the Address box and press the **<Enter>** key to navigate to the Web site.

3. Briefly view the Web site. Point out how this page offers weather information for many cities across the nation and world. The students will be finding weather information for their city or town using this site.

4. Point out the search engine. Explain to the students that they must type a city and state in this search engine to find information for their city or town. (**Note:** This Web site may not offer weather information for small towns. You may need to type the name of a nearby city to obtain weather information.) Type the appropriate city and state and click the search button.

5. When the information appears, discuss the daily temperature information. Discuss the current *temperature* if the information is available. Ask the students what temperature means, and why there is a daily high temperature and a daily low temperature listed.

6. Distribute the *Weather Log* page and briefly discuss it with the students. Complete the *Web site name, URL, My city or town,* and *high temperature* and *low temperature* lines together.

7. Discuss the current weather conditions and point out the symbols on the Web page that show conditions such as sunny, cloudy, rainy, etc. Instruct the students to draw the symbol showing the current weather conditions on their *Weather Log* pages. Then the students should circle the word describing the weather conditions or write a different word next to *other:*.

8. Each day of the week for a couple of weeks, allow the students to log on to the Internet and complete a *Weather Log* page. **Note:** If computer access is limited, allow one or two students to look up the daily weather information each day for the class. You may choose to have a different student or pair of students do this each day.

 # Daily Weather *(cont.)*

Extension Ideas

- Look up the weather information for a few major cities around the country and compare the temperatures and conditions in those cities to your local weather. Ask the students what the people in the other cities might be wearing to keep warm or cool and compare this to what the students are wearing. Challenge the students to find the differences in daily high temperatures between the cities. For older students, plot the daily high temperatures of each city on a single graph (using a different color for each city) to compare the temperatures.

- Discuss basic weather terms such as *forecast, weather conditions, partly cloudy, mostly cloudy, overcast, mostly clear, foggy, showers, rainfall, freezing rain, hail, sleet, ice storm, muggy, lightning, thunder, thunderstorm, blizzard, hurricane, heat wave, fair, flood, drought, hurricane, tornado, twister, snowflake, storm, seasons,* and *thermometer.*

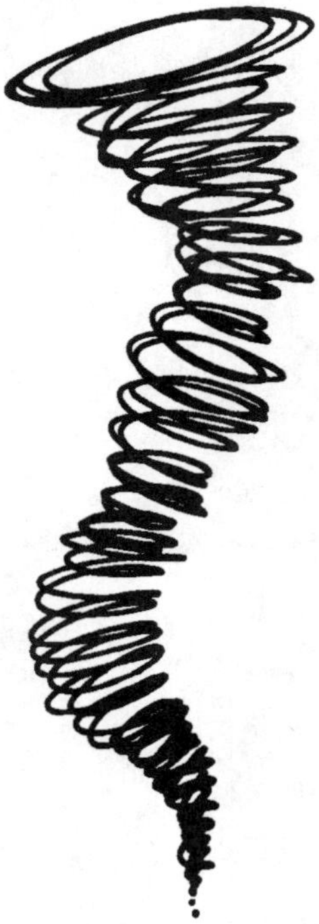

 Weather Log

Web site name: _____

URL: _____

My city or town: _____

The high temperature today will be _____ degrees Fahrenheit.

The low temperature today will be _____ degrees Fahrenheit.

The weather outside looks

sunny   cloudy   rainy   snowy   other: _____

KWL Chart

What We **K**now	What We **W**ant to Know	What We **L**earned

Concept Map

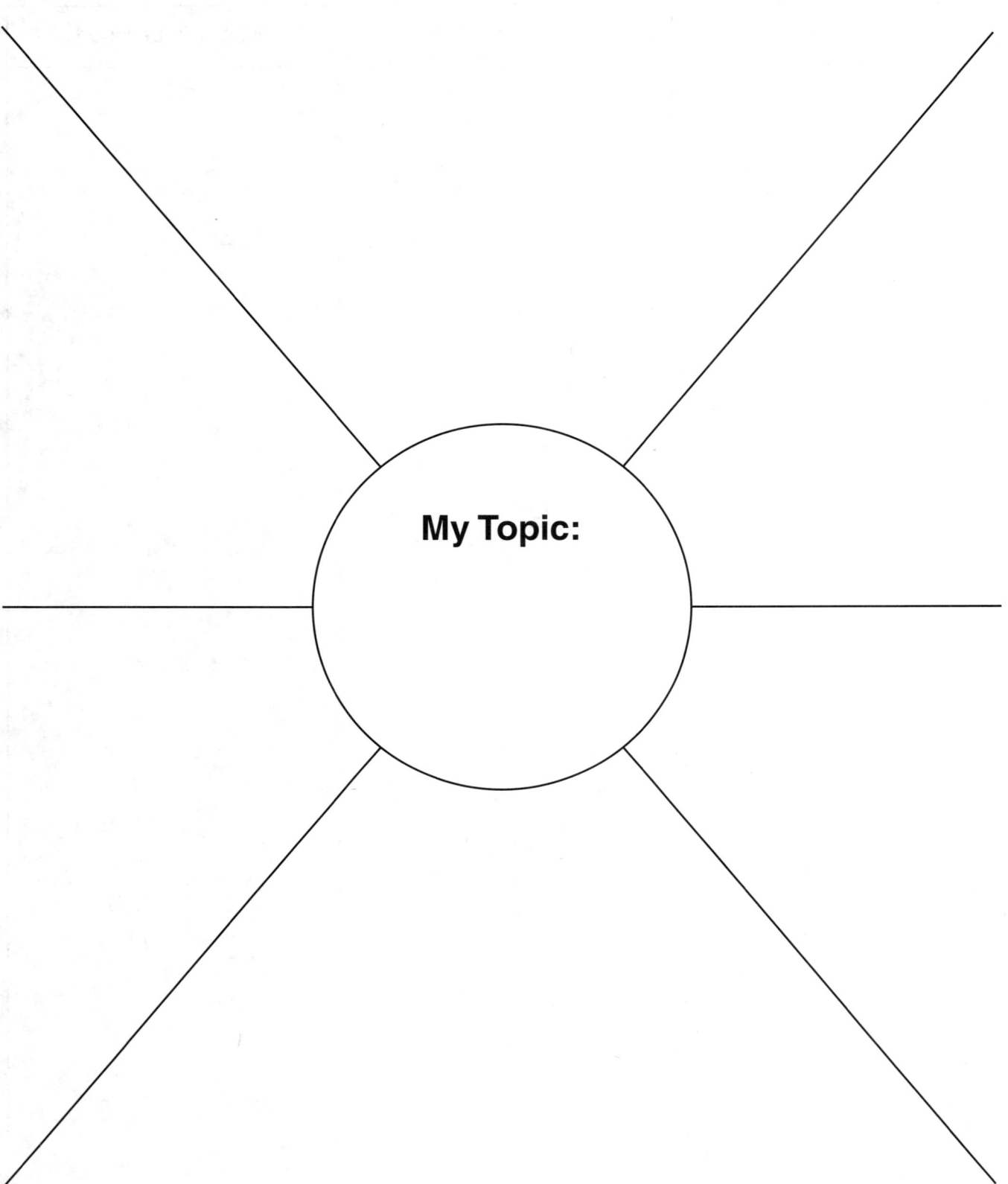

My Topic:

© *Teacher Created Materials, Inc.*

Who, What, Where, and When

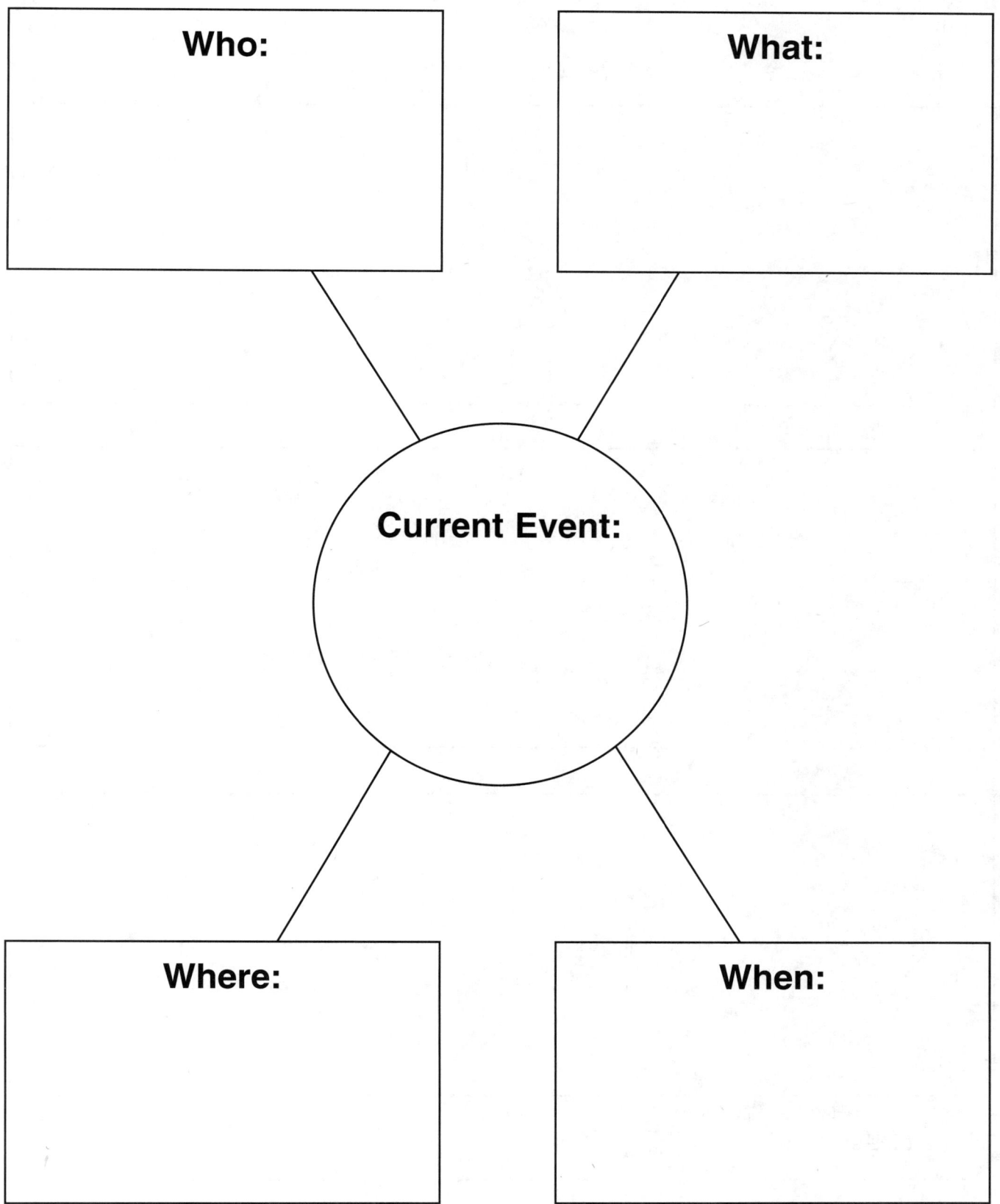

Who:

What:

Current Event:

Where:

When:

Story Mapping

Story Title:

Author:

Beginning

Middle

End

The part I liked best
is_____because_____.

Glossary

Acceptable Use Policy (AUP)—A school district policy regulating proper use of district computers, the network, and the Internet. Parents, students, and teachers must sign AUP forms before using the district computer resources.

Advanced search—A more specific and directed search of Web sites using a search engine.

Attachments—Documents, graphics, or movie clips generated on a computer that are sent with, or "attached," to an e-mail message.

Bookmark—A "saved" Web site. When you bookmark a Web site, you save it to the Favorites menu (*Microsoft Internet Explorer*) or Bookmarks menu (*Netscape Navigator*), to be readily accessible later.

Chat board—A Web page where you can read threads of ongoing conversations about many topics. Chat boards are usually specific to a field or interest, and anyone can join in the discussion by reading other people's posts and replying.

Chat room—A chat room is a meeting place for people who have scheduled an online conversation. Usually anyone who logs in can join the chat.

Cyberspace—The "universe" of computer communications.

Download—To save a file on the Internet to your computer. Technically, it is transferring data from a remote computer to your computer.

E-mail—Short for electronic mail, which is a typed message sent over the Internet. E-mail is usually a component part of the Internet service provided by companies such as *America Online* or *EarthLink*.

Emoticons—Human expressions created from keyboard characters, such as :-) (smiley face).

E-pal—A student with whom another student can correspond using e-mail.

FAQ—Short for Frequently Asked Questions. Many Web sites have a list of FAQs.

Internet filter—A software program that prevents unacceptable Web sites from being viewed on a computer or network of computers.

Home Page—The main or introductory page of a Web site. It is often the first page viewed when visiting a Web site.

HTML—Stands for Hypertext Markup Language. It is the coding language typically used for creating Web pages. With the advent of software programs and Internet sites that allow anyone to create a Web page, knowledge of HTML code is no longer necessary to create a Web page.

Glossary *(cont.)*

HTTP—Stands for Hypertext Transport Protocol. This protocol allows for the movement of hypertext files across the Internet. Note that most Web site addresses begin with *http://*.

Hypertext and Hyperlink—Text or graphics that when clicked, take the user to another Web page, Web site, or different part of the same page.

Internet—A worldwide network of smaller computer networks which offers data and information sharing, e-mail communication, online commerce, and online activities.

Internet Browser—The software program that allows computer users to view Web sites. The two most common browsers are *Microsoft Internet Explorer* and *Netscape Navigator*.

Listserv—An e-mail mailing list of people who share common professional concerns, interests, or personal hobbies.

Live chat—A live chat is a scheduled online conversation about a certain topic, usually featuring an expert in the field to whom you can address questions.

Log On/Log Off—To connect to or disconnect from an Internet Service Provider or computer network.

Modem—The device that uses phone lines or cable to connect your computer to distant computers.

Navigate—To enter Web site addresses or use hyperlinks to locate specific Web sites and information on the Internet.

Netiquette—Etiquette for e-mail and Internet communication.

Netizen—A citizen of the Internet.

Offline—Not connected to a computer network.

Online—Connected to a computer network. It usually refers to being on the Internet.

Posting—Sending a message to a chat board.

Search engine—A feature on a Web site that allows you to conduct a search of a large database of Web sites.

Service provider—A company or organization that offers access to the Internet.

Scavenger hunt—Using a search engine such as Yahooligans.com to find answers to questions or to collect facts on various Web sites.

Glossary *(cont.)*

Truncate—To shorten a Web site address (URL) to its home page address.

Upload—To place a file originally on a single computer or local network on the Internet.

URL—Uniform Resource Locator, or more simply, a Web site address. Example: **http://teachercreated.com**.

Username—Characters and numbers used to identify an individual user of a computer system.

Web quest—Using a home page (usually teacher-created) containing several hyperlinks to visit pre-selected Web sites and to find specific information.

Web page—A single hypertext page within a Web site.

Web site—A hypertext document on the Internet comprised of one or more Web pages.

World Wide Web (The Web, WWW)—The part of the Internet most used today that is composed of millions of hypertext documents that are easily accessible with Internet browsers such as *Microsoft Internet Explorer*.

Bibliography

Cyber Crew Copyright Committee, *Get the Facts*, 1998-2000, *http://www.cyber-crew.com/copyright*

Hopkins, Gary, *Getting Started on the Internet: Add YOUR Name to a Listserv — TODAY!*, Education World, 1998, **http://www.education-world.com/a_curr/curr062.shtml**

Magid, Lawrence J., *Child Safety on the Information Highway, National Center for Missing and Exploited Children*, 1998, **www.safekids.com/child_safety.htm**

Shea, Virginia, "The Core Rules of Netiquette," from the book *Netiquette*, Albion Books, 1994-2000, ISBN: 0-9637025-1-3, **http://www.albion.com/netiquette/**

Starr, Linda, *The Educator's Guide to Copyright and Fair Use*, Education World, 2000, **http://www.education-world.com/a_curr/curr280.shtml**

Templeton, Brad, *10 Big Myths about Copyright Explained*, **http://www.templetons.com/brad/copymyths.html**

Notes

Notes

© Teacher Created Materials, Inc.